My Church

Reprinted 1998, 2002
First published 1957
Revised and updated 1994
Copyright © by Harvest Publications
Arlington Heights, Ill.

ISBN: 0-935797-34-3

Contents

Preface

It is encouraging to know this book has endured for four decades. It was first published in 1957 as the first leadership training manual for the Baptist General Conference. It soon was used by pastors and other church leaders for new members' classes and to help people better understand the Baptist Church. In some cases it became part of instruction in classes in seminary and Bible colleges. Its use went beyond the confines of the Baptist General Conference and the boundaries of the United States.

Some revision was done in 1973. In later years modest updating of statistics was done. Because of the continued demand for the book, it seemed wise to the publishers to make a more complete revision. Though the basic doctrinal positions in the text remain the same, the conditions in the church and in society have significantly changed. I have attempted to reflect some of those changes as they impinge on the various issues dealt with in the text.

It is my prayerful concern that our Lord may continue to use the book in the thinking of many people who wish to better understand the Baptist Church. It is my further hope that it may be useful to many Baptists beyond the Baptist General Conference. The book has been written with that in mind.

The title, *My Church,* has a twofold meaning and purpose. Jesus said, "I will build *my church.*" It is His church. "My church" is His statement. That must be kept clearly in mind as the primary emphasis of the book. Further, as a Baptist I can say with joy and celebration, "This is *my church,*" as I contemplate the teachings of this book. The title suggests the divine-human quality of the church. It belongs to our Lord. He indwells the church. But we human beings are the church. That is the glory of the church.

A work like this is always the result of the input of many people who have shared in the task. Wide reading, personal involvement in the life of the church, interaction with church leaders of many different communions and intentional interviews have influenced the writing of the book. It would be impossible to acknowledge all who have contributed helpful insights over the years.

Some persons need to be acknowledged for contributions in the current revision of this book. Bob Putman of Harvest Publications has contributed in significant ways in his editorial work on the text. John Cionca of Bethel Seminary did a careful review of the text and made many valuable suggestions and corrections. Leith Anderson was most gracious in reviewing the manuscript and writing the introduction. My wife, Alta, put the manuscript on the computer and made some editorial suggestions along the way. Interviews with several pastors gave insight into the work of the church from a practical perspective. To all of these and others I am most grateful. It is my prayer that the book will continue to find a wide readership and be helpful to many in better understanding the church.

Introduction

Around the world there are Baptist churches ranging in size from two or three people to tens of thousands. The largest Protestant denomination in the United States is Baptist. Baptists meet in rented facilities, living rooms, jungle clearings and cathedral-like church buildings. Baptists are among the most inclusive of denominations in race, language and socio-economic position. We are a diverse people.

Perhaps it is too easy to see our differences, although there is great strength in Baptist diversity and flexibility. Don't be deceived by the differences. There is a central core of Baptist beliefs and practices which unite most of us as born-again Christians. We have gathered into local churches with a high commitment to Jesus Christ as our Savior and Lord and to the Bible as our rule for faith and practice.

My Church enables the truth and traditions of Baptists to continue and strengthen. This is not a "book of order" as some denominations have. Nor is it an argument to persuade persons of other denominations to become Baptists. This is a gracious but strong guidebook for understanding how Baptists have carefully turned the teachings of the Bible into the practices of church life.

Gordon Johnson is specially qualified to be our guide. He has pastored churches from Montclair, New Jersey, to San Diego, California. As the Dean of Bethel Theological Seminary in St. Paul, Minnesota, he taught a generation of seminarians who turned into pastors, missionaries and leaders of Baptist churches across North America and around the world. Especially helpful is his sense of history and tradition coupled with an awareness of current trends and issues. He is comfortable that Baptist principles continue while churches change; methods are updated while proven practices stay the same.

As you read the following thirteen chapters, consider some practical advice:

1. *Keep the Bible first.* *My Church* is not the Bible. It is a resource to help apply the Bible to Baptist churches. Where there are Bible references, read and study them for yourself. Constantly return to the Bible as the Word of God for both Christians and the church. In other words, read with *My Church* in one hand and the Bible in the other hand.

2. *Decide for yourself.* You will see that a strong belief of Baptists is that we are each individually responsible before God. Don't believe because the author says so. Don't read with detachment that says, "I'm just doing this for an assignment." Make your own careful and prayerful choices which will turn information into conviction.

3. *Compare to your church* You will find differences. Every church varies. Resolve to discover your own congregation in the light of the Bible and the insights of this book. Expect that some differences may make you uncomfortable. With Christian love and tolerance, be prepared to accept differences while you serve as God's agent to continually align your church with God's Word.

Finally, take delight in sharing fellowship with tens of millions of Baptists around the world today and through history. Together we live for the glory of God in every generation.

Leith Anderson
Eden Prairie, Minnesota

1

The Church's Source of Strength

The church is an amazing organization. It has survived and thrived throughout the ages. It has been persecuted and oppressed, but it has not been obliterated. It has suffered from external enemies and from internal chaos at times, but it still endures.

We have witnessed this in the twentieth century in dramatic ways. The Communist regime in the Eastern bloc countries suppressed the church for seventy years. The Nazi rulers in Germany from 1933 to 1945 either utilized collaborators in the church or persecuted those in the church who opposed the atrocities they imposed on society. Today in both areas the church has survived and is thriving.

A recent survey conducted by the National Opinion Research Center at the University of Chicago, in conjunction with the Russian Center for Public Opinion Research in Moscow, came up with astounding results. Questionnaires were collected from 2964 respondents in 1991. They showed that a religious revival unparalleled in modern history is sweeping Russia. After seven decades in an atheist state, three out of four Russians expressed absolute or great confidence in the church. That is a confidence rating nearly twice as high as Americans report. Twenty-two percent, including nearly a third of those under age 25, said they once were atheists but now believe in God.

This is one of the most enormous swings ever in the history of Christianity. It is a demonstration of the strength of the church. It was oppressed. It was persecuted. Yet it has survived and is now thriving. This is only one illustration of the power of the church.

How do we account for the strength of the church? Any ordinary institution would have died. Any human organization would not have had the stamina to endure the opposition and pressure that the church has endured. Where does the church get its power? That is what this chapter is about.

The place of the Bible

The strength of the church derives from an authority beyond itself. Its enduring quality is not based on clever organization or creative human endeavors. There is a power beyond the earthly element to make the church what it is. That power is the authority of the Bible.

Let us take a look at this book.

First, notice the *adequacy* of the Bible. It gives us enough truth for our faith and life. It is adequate because it is divinely inspired. Even a casual observation of the book amazes us. Simple facts about the Bible thrill us with its glory. It was written over a period of about 1500 years by about forty different writers from varied backgrounds. Yet in all of it there is a sense of unity. That unity may be observed in several ways. The activity of God as Creator God of all things is observed throughout the Bible. The work of God in selecting and guiding His chosen people Israel runs as a thread through the Scriptures. God's activity in Christ was prepared for in the Old Testament and fulfilled in the New Testament. God was working in and through His own people in the Old Testament and then continued that work in and through His church in the New Testament.

The action of God in reconciling human beings to Himself is the main theme of the Bible. The message of this book has changed the lives of people and societies through the ages, and we are compelled to say, "Only the Spirit of God could have given a book like this." The writers were guided by the Spirit as they wrote. The Bible really becomes God's personal letter to us as human beings. He speaks to us and His church through it.

We realize that not all parts of the Bible have the same importance, and yet all parts are equally inspired. We see an illustration of this in the physical world. Eyes are of far greater importance to the human body than tonsils, but both are part of the body God has created. Certain parts of God's Word are of greater importance to the life of the church than other parts, yet all of it is equally inspired. This book is a sufficient guide for church life and for our personal lives.

Second, note the Bible's *certainty.* Scientific and philosophic theories are always subject to revision. So are church creeds and dogmas (authoritative statements of beliefs and doctrines), which have been changed throughout the ages. But the Word of God abides. It is certain. It is unchangeable. We may discover more truth within it, and we may see new slants upon the truth it contains, but the truth that is here has been given once and for all. Jesus said, "Heaven and earth will pass away, but my words will never pass away" (Matthew 24:35). This certainty of the Bible gives us confidence in our Christian experience and in the function of the church.

Third, note the Bible's *authority.* The Bible speaks with an authority present in no other book or literature in the world. This is not due to anything external. No court made it so by decree or decision. The early church councils in the second, third and fourth centuries did not make it so. They turned to it to discover the basis for those creeds and dogmas which they desired to make authoritative for the church.

One writer says, "They simply recognized the authority of the book itself. The formation of Scripture under God took care of itself. It was inevitable that this dynamic and mighty literature would come together in a vital and organic unity since it was all created by one common life and power of God."

There is an inner power within this book that forces itself on human beings. It is a divine message that cannot be avoided. Martin Luther, the great Protestant Reformer, found himself forced to commit to the authority of the Scriptures rather than to the church or its leadership. The more he examined the Word of God, his own convictions, and his relationship to the Lord and to the church, the more he was forced to reject the Pope's statements as equally authoritative to the Bible. He did not want to leave the church. He wanted to abide by the Pope and by the councils. But finally, in the midst of his struggle with truth, he was pressed into a corner. He had to admit that the councils and the Popes had erred. Because of this he took his stand on the authority of the Word of God.

He gave this testimony when he was on trial: "Unless I am convinced by the testimony of Scripture or by an evident reason—for I confide neither in the Pope nor a council alone, since it is certain that they have often erred and contradicted themselves—I am held fast by the Scriptures adduced by me, and my conscience is taken captive by God's Word. I neither can nor will revoke anything seeing that it is not safe or right to act against my conscience. I can do no other. God help me. Amen."

No other book is authoritative for the church or for any true religion. Other religions have their books, such as Mormonism with its *Book of Mormon*. Mary Baker Eddy, the founder of Christian Science, wrote *Science and Health with Key to the Scriptures* in 1875. The implication of her title is that the Scriptures were a lost treasure until her interpretation. This implication is contrary to all we know about the Bible and what God has done for humankind. We do not need special human keys to understand the essential message which God gives to responsible persons through the Scriptures.

The Bible is the authority for the function of the church. It guides the life of the church. But above all, the Bible points us to Christ, the Living Word of God. Speaking to the Pharisees and scribes, Jesus said, "You diligently study the Scriptures because you think that by them you possess eternal life. These are the Scriptures that testify about me, yet you refuse to come to me to have life" (John 5:39-40).

The ultimate purpose of the written Word of God is to point us to Jesus Christ, the Living Word. He is the one who is the head of the church and is the one who transforms each of us who trusts in Him. That makes the Bible vital to us and to the church.

The place of tradition

Though the Bible is the sole authority for the faith and life of the church, as well as for us as individuals, there are two other areas that must be considered. These are tradition and practicality. Both of these are important in considering the strength of the church, though both must always be subservient to the authority of the Bible.

Tradition has to do with the historical roots out of which the church has come. There is considerable historical similarity among the various denominations. That is especially true of early periods in the development of the church. The work, decisions and writings of leaders and councils throughout church history have been highly important. All Christians acknowledge this. Out of the work of leaders and church councils have come creeds (authoritative statements of foundational beliefs) and statements of faith. These have formed the basis of church tradition.

These creeds and statements of faith impact some of the denominations that are prominent in our society today.

Some church groups claim to be non-creedal. That means these denominations do not allow any statement of faith or doctrine to be authoritative over them. Their claim is that the authority for them is the Bible and especially the New Testament. These non-creedal churches accept the early creeds produced by the church councils as valid statements of doctrine as understood from the Scriptures. These churches also utilize their own affirmations of faith, but they quickly affirm that the Scriptures are primary and are the ultimate authority for them. Among the non-creedal churches are the United Methodist Church, the United Church of Christ, the Evangelical Free Church, the Evangelical Covenant Church, the Christian Missionary and Alliance Church and the Christian Church, as well as Baptists.

Creedal churches are those who turn to particular creeds or confessions of faith as the basis for their faith and activity. All turn to the ancient creeds, but each denomination has developed its own confession of faith. All will say that the Bible is authoritative, but also that these confessions are very important for the life of the church. Among the creedal churches are the Lutheran Church, the Episcopal Church, the Church of England, the Christian Reformed Church, the Presbyterian Church and the Roman Catholic Church.

When we speak of creeds and confessions (statements of faith), we are talking about tradition. It is related to history. These statements of doctrine were produced at different points in history as expressions of the church's understanding of the teachings of the Bible. As each of these churches developed in history, they produced their own confessions of faith to particularize their own group. Their confessions make each of them distinct. These have to do with tradition.

The Roman Catholic Church is more guided by tradition than any other segment of the Christian church. Catholics believe that the successor to the apostle Peter is the Pope. They base this understanding on several statements to Peter by the Lord Jesus (Matthew 16:18-19; Luke 22:31-32; John 21:15-19). All of the leaders of the Catholic Church are considered successors to the apostles, with the same authority. A Catholic study book says: "The bishops, with the Pope, are the ones who teach and guide the church. They must serve the people of God and the world by proclaiming and guarding the message of Christ amongst us. They are the successors of the apostles whom Christ commissioned to 'teach all nations'."

The Catholic Church places high significance on the actions of leaders and councils throughout its history to determine its doctrine and activities. The Bible is authoritative for the Catholic Church, but its approach to the Bible is different from that of Protestants. Their view can probably be best understood by a statement from this same study book: "Catholics and Protestants... have the utmost regard and respect for the Word of God, but each approaches it somewhat differently. Catholics believe that the Bible needs to be guarded by the teaching authority of the church. Thus in her creed she provides us with a sort of dictionary of the Bible. We believe that the Bible is the heart of the tradition of the church and without the church to hand it on, the Bible would lose most of its power.

"The Catholic sees the Bible as the Book once and for all written by the church, for the church, and how, separated from the church, it can easily be misunderstood."

When we see that approach in relating the Scriptures to tradition, we are able to better understand how some doctrines not clearly taught within the Bible become the dogma of the Catholic Church. Though the Bible is authoritative, it came through the church and is understood best within the church. That means that decisions made by the church hold equal authority with doctrines seen clearly in the Bible. That is how the infallibility of the Pope when he speaks with church authority could have been determined as a dogma of the church in 1870, and the Assumption of Mary was settled in 1950. This is the doctrine that Mary was taken up into heaven following her death, as Jesus was.

Baptists are a non-creedal people. But Baptists are also a people with a history. They find great value in creeds and in the decisions of the ecumenical councils in the early history of the church. Their basic understanding of the crucial biblical doctrines comes from the decisions of those councils. They have utilized confessions of faith at various periods in their history. Many local Baptist churches adopt their own affirmations of faith. Some Baptist denominations have utilized statements of faith as guidelines for determining membership in the fellowship as well as directing the function of the churches.

As an example, the Baptist General Conference adopted an Affirmation of Faith in 1951. These formal statements of beliefs are used to give expression to its current understanding of the teachings of Scripture. They help people outside the church understand what a local church or a denominational fellowship believes the Scriptures teach.

Although Baptists are not creedal, they recognize the value of their heritage and the development of doctrinal understandings in the past. And they also need to recognize the place of affirmations of faith as guidelines for the function of the church.

But such affirmations of faith cannot become laws that supersede the Bible. The Bible is our sole authority for faith and function. The official creeds must be used only as interpreters of Scripture.

A local church may use an affirmation to help prospective members to understand what that church believes the Bible teaches. Some prospective members may disagree. It may even be necessary for the local church to refuse membership to such persons. That would not be an inconsistent act for the church to do. It is merely saying to these prospective members that they would not feel at home in the church since their understanding of biblical teaching is in conflict with that of the church.

But we must always keep before us that we are under the authority of the Bible. All statements of creed must be subservient to the Scriptures. In talking with the Pharisees and scribes about the relation of Himself and His disciples to tradition, Jesus said, "You have a fine way of setting aside the commands of God in order to observe your own traditions" (Mark 7:9).

The place of practicality

The other element that must be considered in respect to the strength of the church is doing what is practical.

Throughout its history the church on many occasions has had to make decisions about the life of the church on the basis of expediency rather than the use of any other criteria. At times these decisions were legitimate and right. At other times such decisions have been in violation of scriptural support or historical precedent.

Take, for example, baptism. It is agreed by most in all denominations that the practice of baptism in the New Testament and in the early church was by immersion of the believer in water. As the ceremony mistakenly became more and more associated with the salvation experience, problems arose when it was impossible to immerse a person because of ill health or other circumstances. Gradually the method was shifted to pouring water over the body and then to sprinkling, because these modes were more practical. It was Karl Barth, a Swiss Reformed Church theologian and probably the greatest theologian in our century, who said: "One can hardly deny that baptism carried out as immersion—as it was in the West until well on into the Middle Ages—showed what was represented in far more expressive fashion than did the affusion [pouring] which later became customary, especially when this affusion was reduced from a real wetting to a sprinkling and eventually in practice to a mere moistening with as little water as possible." The decision that sprinkling become an authoritative doctrine was based on practicality. Though it is now the form used by the majority of the segments of the Christian church, it was gradual in development.

In more recent years, N.P. Williams of Oxford became disturbed because he could not find evidence of infant baptism in the New Testament. Thus, he felt led to plead that men should "trust the instincts of the historic church." This is an admission that the authority for the change in the method of baptism came through the pragmatic decision of the post-New Testament church.

An illustration from my own life might make more graphic the use of practicality in church life. While I was pastoring a city church, a woman called my wife on the telephone. She presented an excellent scheme whereby the people of our church could earn a great deal of money.

When told that we did not support our church by selling things, she could not understand it.

"Don't you need money?" she asked.

My wife answered, "Certainly we do."

"Well, then how do you get your money?"

My wife explained that members of our church believed in giving a tithe of their income to the Lord and His work.

The woman asked, "What is that? How do you spell it?"

So my wife spelled "tithe" and explained what it meant.

The woman said, "Why, the only place I have ever heard of that is in the Bible. I have never heard of a church that followed that method."

Striking, isn't it? She had heard of tithing only in the Bible—she hadn't heard of any church doing it. The Bible is the authority for the church, yet many do not take it seriously as the standard for their church's faith and actions.

It is easy to allow human reason and good common sense to become the authoritative criterion for decisions about the church's faith and activities. It takes effort and care to discover the biblical principle behind decisions made in the church.

In recent years, some have questioned the authority of the Bible. They want to accept only some basic beliefs such as God's love for human beings and the necessity of loving one's neighbors. From then on specific decisions are left to one's own judgment. Here we face a fluctuating authority because humanity's understanding changes.

However, we can't dispense with all practicality within the church. We must guide the activities of the church in a world with far different conditions than existed in the New Testament period. But the principles found in the New Testament are complete enough to guide us in all our decisions. Some things are needed today that are not specifically outlined in the Bible. For instance, most states require that churches have trustees or some other designated officers to care for the church's legal matters.

Though trustees are not found in the New Testament, their office is not contrary to New Testament principles.

Our guiding rule in church matters is to follow the teaching of the New Testament. When we believe it necessary to add something not specifically mentioned within the New Testament, we make certain the addition does not violate New Testament principles.

The strength of the church results from its adherence to the authority of the Bible. As the church relies on the Bible as its guide in its faith and work, it becomes strong. It is this that has made the church able to endure and thrive. I visited the church in Moscow in 1966 when it was greatly restricted under a tyrannical atheistic, Communistic rule. The church remained strong in spite of the restrictions. How were new leaders being trained, I asked. They had no seminaries or Bible school. They responded with another question: "How much do your students read the Bible?" Their students, studying individually with a mature pastor, would read the Bible through as many as 35 times. This was the secret of the power of the church behind the Iron Curtain. The Bible is the church's authority and power.

2

What Does Church *Mean?*

Alex Haley's book, *Roots*, published in 1974, traced his history as an African American. The book and subsequent TV miniseries triggered a new interest in many people to discover their roots. Dozens of businesses sprang up to help people investigate their origins. In similar manner many people today are curious about the church. Where did the church come from? How did it come into being? Who was its founder? How did it develop?

Its beginning

It all began in the first century. Jesus was the first to use the word as we know it today. He said in Matthew 16:18: "I will build my church." It is well to note the circumstances that led Him to speak as He did. All of Jesus' preaching and teaching was occasional. What He taught or preached was prompted by events and surrounding situations. For example, on one occasion Jesus asked the apostles about people's opinions of Him, now that He was becoming well-known. They told Him some considered Him to be one of the ancient prophets. He then asked them what they thought. Peter immediately replied, "You are the Christ, the Son of the living God." With that Jesus said, "You are Peter, and on this rock I will build my church."

Now what does this mean? Who is the rock on whom He would build His church? There are three primary interpretations: 1) Rock refers to Peter. 2) Rock refers to Jesus Christ. 3) Rock refers to Peter's statement of belief.

On careful examination it appears that a proper interpretation is a combination of all three. Jesus said, "You are Peter [*Petros*], and on this rock [*petra*] I will build my church." It is obvious there is a play on words here. Jesus is saying, "Your name is Rock, and on this rock I will build my church." On what basis did Jesus make this statement? It was based on Peter's discovery and confession of Jesus' real identity. Peter said, "You are the Christ." How did Peter come to that conclusion? It came to him as divine revelation. "This was not revealed to you by man, but by my Father in heaven" (v. 17). Peter's own ability had not brought him to that conclusion. The Lord made it known to him. Thus, our Lord could build His church on Peter and continue to build it on others who have made the same discovery and declaration of faith in Jesus Christ.

Let us reflect on some truths we learn from our Lord's words. First, He is the *church's foundation*. He is the One who said, "*I* will build my church." He will build it on human beings like Peter who have also made the discovery that Jesus is the Christ, the Son of the living God. But it is He who reveals Himself to people. It is He who does the building. In 1 Corinthians 3:11 He is called the foundation. Ephesians 2:20 says the church is "built on the foundation of the apostles and prophets, with Christ Jesus himself as the chief cornerstone." Again in 1 Peter 2:6-8 Christ is called the cornerstone. Jesus Christ is clearly the foundation and cornerstone of the church.

Jesus is *Lord* of the church. He said, "I will build *my* church." The church belongs to Him. He started it. He changes all those who accept His free gift of salvation, and they become part of His church. He continues the church, and by His power He is the motivation that expands the church. He is the Lord.

Metaphors in the New Testament graphically speak of His lordship. He is the Head of the body. The body cannot function apart from the head. As the Cornerstone of the building, He is the central figure of the church. He is the Vine, and we are the branches. He is the Shepherd of the flock, and we follow Him. He is the Bridegroom, and the church is the bride. These metaphors clearly show that Jesus Christ is Master over the church. The church that recognizes this will be powerful and effective

The church is *permanent.* The Lord said, "The gates of Hades will not overcome it." The church will be opposed, and the opposition will not come from ordinary human sources. It will come from spiritual forces. Hell, Satan and all his cohorts will oppose the church and all of its work, but those who are in the church are on the winning team. Though we sometimes feel insignificant in our task because we may be a small minority in our community, our church will eventually be victorious as it is true to its Lord and His Word.

Finally, we observe another truth that comes from our Lord's second and final use of the term in Matthew 18:17. It suggests the necessary *local aspect* of the church. Here He refers to a dispute between two believers that cannot be resolved. The dispute should then be brought to the church. It would be impossible to bring a matter of dispute to the universal church. It would have to be brought to a local group. The practical activity of the church He founded demands a local fellowship.

Its meaning

When we use the word "church" various images come to mind. For some it suggests a denomination like the Roman Catholic Church or the Presbyterian Church. For others it means a building that can be identified as a particular church. Many identify the church as a group of people. When the word was first used as we know it today, it was used by the Goths, who came down from the north into the Roman Empire. They observed Christians at worship. They saw them in small groups in their houses of worship, so their first conception of the church was the building where the believers met. It was the tangible, physical expression of Christianity that they noticed, and thus they spoke of the church with primary emphasis on the place of meeting.

The origin of the word is actually from the Greek word *kuriakon*, which suggests the building. It means "belonging to a lord or master." For most people we continue to use the word church to designate the building where worship and other activities are conducted. Though that is the word used in our English translations of the Bible, it is not the word used in the Greek New Testament. *Kuriakon* is never used in the New Testament for church. The word is *ecclesia*, which means "the assembly of called out ones."

The word *ecclesia* emphasizes not the building in which believers met, but *the believers themselves*. The church was the assembly of people who believed in Christ, whether they met in a cave, in a house, in a synagogue or out in the open. The people of New Testament times were quite aware of the significance of the word when it was used.

The word *ecclesia* came from the Greek's city-state government. It was used of the assembly of citizens as they gathered together to make laws and to enact special legislation for their own city. Four facts that help explain the New Testament church were found in this Greek city assembly.

First, the Greek assembly was a local group. It did not involve a whole country or an empire. The men gathered together to represent that one city.

Second, the group was autonomous. They ruled independently in the local situation, but sensed a relationship to other areas.

Third, membership in the group assumed definite qualifications. Citizens had to meet particular criteria before they were considered voting members.

Fourth, the Greek assembly was conducted on democratic principles. They voted as a democratic body and the majority ruled.

These four principles were meaningful guidelines in the function of the New Testament church.

In the Roman Empire when each group of Roman citizens gathered (wherever it might be), their assembly was a voice of Rome. This group had no meaning apart from Rome. Each Roman citizen arriving in a city where such a group existed automatically became a member of that assembly. Geographically these groups could be several thousand miles from Rome, but they were still a vital part of Rome. William Barclay, the well-known Bible commentator and author, said, "That is the true idea of the church; each local church is only a part, a miniature of the great universal church."

Both the local and the broader relationships must be kept in perspective as we examine the New Testament emphasis on the church.

Its biblical use

It is well to examine the use of the word "church" in the Bible. The idea is seen in the Old Testament when it refers to the assembly of the people of God. But because the church really began in the New Testament era, it is best to study how the word was used in the New Testament. The New Testament always uses the same word whether referring to the total community or the local congregation.

The word is found 112 times. Twelve times it refers to the universal church—that is, to the church made up of all believers in Jesus Christ no matter where they might be found, in what era or in what denominational group. Ninety times the word clearly refers to a local assembly. The other times it speaks of a collective sense that usually refers to a visible church.

Based on these numbers alone, the primary meaning of the church seems to be the local, visible expression of it. The fellowship and function of the local group was very important. It was here that Christian growth and vital witness occurred. On the other hand, group members also sensed a oneness with other believers a distance away. They consulted with one another. They sought each other's encouragement. Notice the interdependence expressed in the Jerusalem Council in Acts 15.

Though the word universal (or "catholic") is never used in the New Testament, the idea is clearly seen. The letters of Paul to the churches at Ephesus and Colossae indicate the universal aspect of the church. D.W.B. Robinson in the *New Bible Dictionary* says, "While there might be as many churches as there were cities or even households, yet the New Testament recognized only one *ecclesia* without finding it necessary to explain the relationship between the one and the many. The one was not an amalgamation or federation of the many. It was a 'heavenly' reality belonging not to the form of this world but to the realm of resurrection glory where Christ is exalted at the right hand of God."

After Jesus' ascension a group of 120 at Jerusalem gathered together in prayer. Then the Holy Spirit came upon them. After that, they witnessed about Jesus Christ. As a result of prayer, the work of the Holy Spirit and their witness, three thousand were added to the church at Jerusalem. Behind the formation and expansion of the church we find prayer, the work of the Holy Spirit and witnessing about Christ. This principle was true in the organization of all the groups of believers in the early church period. The growing church was not the result of hyper-organization. It was the work of individuals and groups of believers who came together in prayer, who sensed the power of the Holy Spirit and who witnessed to Jesus Christ as the Redeemer.

Its Baptistic use

Someone may ask, "How did Baptist churches begin? Who is the founder? What are their roots?" Some people think that the founder is John the Baptist, but few Baptists hold this view. John the Baptist baptized by immersion, but his baptism had a different significance than the baptism which followed the death and resurrection of Jesus Christ. The church had not yet begun when John was baptizing. It began after the death and resurrection of the Lord Jesus.

The Baptist church began, as such, in the sixteenth century during the Reformation period when many other Protestant groups began. The term Baptist was not chosen by the Baptist people themselves. It was originally a nickname in the same manner that the name Christian was first a nickname. Christ's followers did not choose the name "Christian," nor did the Baptists choose the name "Baptist" for themselves. They were first called "Anabaptists," which means rebaptizers. They baptized again those who had been "baptized" in infancy, because they did not believe that such sprinkling was baptism according to the New Testament. They believed that baptism always follows a conversion experience and is accomplished by complete submersion in water.

Baptists do not claim any one individual as their founder. They appreciate the work and contributions of each of the reformers—Martin Luther, John Calvin, Huldrych Zwingli, John Huss, John Knox and others. Though ready to accept many of these men's contributions to biblical study, Baptists turn to the New Testament as their authority for Christian living and church activity.

Baptists believe that the function of the local assembly is of highest significance. Thus, we tend not to speak of our denominational fellowship or any Baptist denomination as "the Baptist Church." It is really Baptist churches in fellowship with one another that make up the larger group. This larger fellowship is necessary to facilitate a worldwide witness, but it remains a fellowship in service for Christ.

Because Baptists emphasize the independence and autonomy of the local assembly, the employed officers of district and national offices are considered servants of the church. Submission to the lordship of Christ is important both in the local churches and among denominational leaders. As the New Testament believers discovered how much they needed one another, we are discovering the same need. We cannot go it alone.

The Baptist General Conference, for example, has its international service center at Arlington Heights, Ill. It has a liberal arts college and a theological seminary in St. Paul, Minn., with a second campus in San Diego, Calif. Member churches are thankful to God for every one of the leaders in these places as well as the leaders in the various districts. These men and women are servants of our churches. They are available for counsel.

They give direction to the total fellowship in growth concerns, instructional help and materials, missionary outreach, and guidelines and counsel in problem situations. We need one another in this larger fellowship. We function more adequately by our interdependence. The same may be observed in other Baptist groups as well.

Each of us should be thrilled to be part of a church of Jesus Christ. As we review the roots out of which we have come, we will sense the high privilege we possess as church members.

3

The Freedom
Which Controls Us

What prompted leaders in the past to guide the church in the way it has developed? What is the driving force that keeps the church developing the way it has today? Is there a basic principle that controls the direction in which the church should move? Is there an underlying controlling principle that keeps the church from negating its effectiveness? We believe there is. It is a principle that arises out of the New Testament as well as out of human experience. It is not a principle that supersedes the New Testament; it is a result of its teaching. This principle is a distinguishing principle for the Baptist church.

Let us seek to define it. It is the inherent right of every person equally with every other person in the world to deal personally and directly with God through Jesus Christ and, therefore, to deal with other persons.

It means that every individual has direct access through Christ to God. No person or group of people or organization can stand between an individual and God. It further means that all people are on an equal plane in the sight of God and in their responsibility to God. To understand this is to understand Baptist practices.

The source of the principle

How do we arrive at this principle of responsible freedom? It first arises out of a *fundamental human characteristic.* Within the human life are fundamental convictions, innate desires and basic drives. One of these innate convictions is that an individual believes he is just as free as any other person. Freedom is a great human passion. From the earliest days of childhood the human being gives expression to this inner desire. God gave us this basic drive. If God gave it, there must be a legitimate way to express it.

A second source is that *man and woman are created in the image of God.* What does this mean? It does not refer to our bodies, for God has no body; therefore, it must involve personality. Our personality includes our intellect, our emotion and our will. In this respect we are in the image of God. One of the primary aspects of personality is will. A will gives a person freedom to make decisions. Thus the fact that man and woman are created in the image of God indicates they have a basic freedom before God.

The third and doubtless most important source of our principle is the *New Testament.* Here we find several reasons this is a basic principle within the life of the church. First, the individual is primary in the New Testament. The Lord in His ministry placed an emphasis on individuals. Note His conversation with the woman at the well in Samaria. He had deep concern for this sinning woman as an individual. The Lord Jesus told a parable about one lost sheep with 99 in the fold. The shepherd was willing to sacrifice energy and time, even risk his life, to reach the one. That puts a premium on the importance of the individual.

Repeatedly the Lord Jesus was involved in personal interviews with individuals. He spoke to throngs of people, He taught them, He fed the multitudes. But in every case where there was need, He dealt with the individual personally. A personal encounter with the Lord Jesus is necessary.

For this reason successful evangelistic movements use many specially trained people to deal individually with those who make decisions. It is the individual that counts. That is New Testament teaching.

The conversion experience breaks down class barriers. We are all on an equal plane in Christ Jesus (Galatians 3:28). One can see a corporation president and a trades-man sitting side by side in a church pew and greet one another warmly following the service. But that is not the test. Go to the church board meeting and see these two contributing and interacting concerning the work of the church. Each is respected for his own contribution. But that is not the whole test. Visit a home where a Bible study is in progress. The same men are present. Listen to the dis-cussion. Hear the prayers uttered. You cannot tell which is the corporation president and which the tradesman. The barriers are gone. Freedom is evident. That is the real expression of the New Testament church with all class dis-tinctions gone.

The New Testament teaches that every believer is a priest before God. This was a new concept. See 1 Peter 2:5,9; Revelation 1:6; 5:10; 20:6. It is called the universal *priest-hood of the believer.* This glorious doctrine, rediscovered in the Protestant Reformation, led to the liberation of the lay people. Each believer discovered he had direct access to God.

What does it mean to be a priest? The primary function of the Old Testament priest was to represent the people before God, to carry the needs of the people to God. Access to God is now available to each Christian. There is no sep-arate priesthood in the New Testament. Jesus broke down the barrier between God and man that made the priest-hood necessary. His death upon the cross rent the veil that separated the priesthood from the people. His death made possible direct access into the presence of God by all who put their trust in Him (Hebrews 10:19-22). Now the only mediator between man and God is Christ Himself (1 Timothy 2:5). No other human mediator is necessary, and none can assume this role. There may be teaching, there may be preaching, but each individual is accountable to God and has the privilege of direct access to God.

Jesus teaches that there should be no interference between the individual and God. In Matthew 23:8-10 we read the clear teaching of our Lord about our relationship to God. None is to be called master. None is to be called father. Christ is the only one who is Master. We are all on one level before God. This was spoken to the multitude and the apostles. The subsequent verses indicate that any who would aspire to leadership must be genuine servants.

The apostles also were convinced of their direct responsibility to the Lord. In Acts 5:29, when they were threatened by the religious leaders, they said, "We must obey God rather than men!" No religious leader could suppress their direct accountability to the Lord.

These reasons clarify the source of this basic principle. It is evident from our human characteristics, from the fact that we are created in the image of God, and particularly from the New Testament. No human interference can prevent the believer's coming directly to God. He is also on an equal basis with all other human beings in this privilege and responsibility.

The effect of the principle

How does this principle of accountable freedom work? What does it do for each of us? What does it do in the life of our church? It is in the function of the principle that we see how glorious is our privilege. It is in the principle's practical outworking that we see some of the differences among various denominations. A correct understanding of this principle will help us appreciate the church so much more. There are eight different areas in which I would like to suggest the practical expression of this principle.

First, it relates to *the Bible*. Think about this. The Bible is God's personal letter to you and me. I may pick it up and read it. It is my privilege to hear God speak to me from it. I may seek another person's help to understand it, but I am completely free to make my own decisions about what it says. I know God has messages for me about my life. He will help me in my decisions. The Bible is open to me to hear His voice. What an outstanding privilege!

This truth is one of the primary reasons for the rapid growth of the Protestant churches during the Reformation. For centuries lay people had not been reading the Bible, and they did not know its message. The Reformation gave the Bible to the people in their own language. As they began to read it, they discovered the message for themselves. It was transforming. The same thing is happening today. A new interest in Bible study, both in homes and in church groups, is bringing renewal to individuals as well as to churches.

Second, it relates to *a person's salvation*. What a crucial issue! To know that I am rightly related to God. To be totally confident that I have eternal life. The privilege of making the decision that will put me in a right relation to God is mine to make. No person can do it for me or keep me from doing it. John 1:12 puts the privilege and responsibility right in my lap. How right and how wholesome!

Many churches teach that salvation depends upon the act of baptism. That would violate this basic truth because it holds that a person would be dependent on a baptizer for salvation. But each individual is accountable to the Lord for himself. Salvation does not even come through the church, though one is likely to understand its meaning through the church. Most decisions of faith in Christ are made in the church or in some agency of the church, but these decisions are still the individual's own choice.

Third, it relates to *baptism*. Most churches today use sprinkling as the form of baptism. Nearly all who are sprinkled are infants. Obviously no infant is able to make his own decision about participating in this rite. This is determined by the parent or some other related person. Someone may ask, "What's the difference between infant baptism and child dedication practiced in our churches?" That ceremony is completely the act of the parent. It does not impart any "grace" or express any feelings on the part of the child. It expresses only the desire of the parents. The parents are longing for God's blessing upon the child, for wisdom in training the child and for His leadership in all that is related to their home. It is proper for the parents to do this, and God has promised His blessing upon the home that honors Him. But in baptism the individual must make his own decision.

Fourth, it relates to *the Lord's Supper* (or the communion service). Here the fact of accountable freedom is also applicable. It is the individual who makes the decision whether or not to participate. Every real believer in Jesus Christ should participate in the Lord's Supper. While instruction should be given about the significance of this ordinance, it is still the responsibility of the individual to decide. No pastor, elder or deacon can go through the congregation and determine who should and who should not participate. The only exception would be when discipline is necessary for known sin. Then such an action should be taken well before the time for participating in the communion fellowship.

Fifth, it relates to *Christian living*. Here we enter troubled waters. Who is to make the decisions about lifestyle matters? The issues involved are not always clear-cut. If standards are imposed by some leaders, we can get caught in legalism which violates our own principle. The individual is responsible to make lifestyle decisions. But those decisions must be made on the basis of forthright biblical guidelines: 1) What will glorify our Lord, 2) What will uplift and not harm other persons, 3) What will contribute to the common good of the church, 4) What contributes to the person's individual growth. The decisions about Christian living are still the individual's decision, but the believer belongs to the Lord, and recognizes personal accountability to Him.

Sixth, it relates to *others*. We are social beings. We live in a world with other people. In these relationships our principle still applies. Because we are responsible to God and have direct access to God, we are also responsible to others. We must share this freedom with them, allowing them to make their own spiritual decisions. We cannot force our faith on others, but each individual has the right to share his or her faith. Baptists will always strive to preserve this right for all no matter what their religious beliefs.

Seventh, it relates to *church government.* The New Testament church was a democracy. That emphasizes our basic principle of accountable freedom. Each individual has as much voice and authority as any other individual within the church. The church is not to be controlled by a hierarchy. Read Matthew 20:25-28; 23:8-12. The pastor or minister of the gospel is a servant, not the father of the flock. The church members vote to call the pastor they believe to be God's leader or shepherd. By its own vote the church acknowledges the leadership of the one they have called. But the pastor's authority depends on submission to the Lord. Ordination does not make a different person out of the pastor. The church ordains a person only as an act of recognition that God has already ordained that one. Thus, within the government of the church each individual, including the pastor, has one vote. Each member is on the same level as every other one.

Eighth, it relates to *church and state.* The liberties that we enjoy in this country are the result of the principle which we are examining. There is a friendly relationship between the church and state, and yet there is separation. This is in harmony with the words of the Lord Jesus in Matthew 22:21. This glorious privilege of freedom and separation of church and state was lost to the church for many centuries. From 313, when Constantine legalized Christianity and united it with the activities of the Empire, until 1638, when Roger Williams established complete liberty in Rhode Island, in every country where the Christian religion prevailed a state church also prevailed. The state supported and thus controlled the activities of the church. This is a violation of the truth of individual freedom. The privilege we now enjoy in our country was purchased with the price of blood and of great sacrifice.

One cannot help but thank God for this glorious principle. We have the privilege of direct access to God. We have the privilege of individual freedom and accountability to God. We have an equal footing with all other human beings in the sight of God. It is a glorious distinctive.

The control of the principle

The truth in which we delight also has its perils. There is danger if freedom is misunderstood to mean license, acting with disregard of biblical and moral restraint. Individual freedom and accountability to God is a privilege that has an accompanying responsibility. Freedom is God-given. That means that freedom can only be expressed properly when it is under His control. It does not mean anarchy. Freedom does not mean license to do as one pleases. Such behavior would destroy freedom.

Our primary control is the *lordship of Jesus Christ.* He is the Authority above the church. He gave the freedom. He must be the One to whom we turn over control of our lives. When we are in submission to Him, we continue to enjoy real freedom, but it does not lose its value by becoming license. Read Philippians 2:9-11 and Colossians 1:18. Christ must have the supremacy in everything. Anything that is contrary to His will would be a violation of the principle.

A second control is *the great commission* to go into all the world making disciples of all peoples (Matthew 28:19-20). The Lord gave the commission to the church to fulfill. That commission was His final statement before He left the earth. It is crucial that it be carried out. Many churches and denominations have incorporated the commission in their purpose statements. Any action by an individual or church to minimize this commission would be a violation of the principle.

A third control is the fact of *the church itself.* The Lord Jesus founded the church. He said in Matthew 16:18 that it was His church. It was founded to carry out the task involved in the great commission. But anything that would hinder the fellowship of this church would be contrary to His will and a violation of the principle. That would apply to the local church as well as the broader expression of the church. Read 1 Corinthians 3:16-17. The "you" in "you are God's temple" is plural, referring to the church. The text indicates that it is a very serious matter to violate God's temple or His church.

The fourth control is *our responsibility to others.* We are social beings. We are in a world of many people, and we depend upon one another and are accountable for one another. Christians do not live in a vacuum. We cannot say as Cain said, "Am I my brother's keeper?" As believers we are our brother's keeper. Our Lord illustrated this clearly in the well-known parable of the good Samaritan (Luke 10:29-38). We also observe it in the writings of Paul in

1 Corinthians 8:12-13 and Galatians 6:2. We are responsible to those about us: responsible as witnesses, responsible as encouraging Christians. We are never free to do anything that would harm another or hinder another from coming to Christ.

Our principle of individual freedom and accountability to God is based on the teaching of the New Testament about the priesthood of believers. In each location in Scripture where the priesthood of believers is mentioned, the term is in the plural. The doctrine does not teach a stark individualism. It teaches a beautiful freedom for each believer in the context of a community. We are responsible to others and for others.

Our glorious freedom will remain a freedom only as long as we permit it to be governed by the controls that have been mentioned. We must be under the lordship of Christ, submissive to the great commission, actively working for the total good of the church and responsible to those about us. We are free, but we must not misuse the freedom. In the measure that we use our freedom, in that measure we keep it. In the measure that we misuse it, in that measure we lose it.

4

What Makes Baptists Distinct

Someone may ask how one can distinguish a Baptist church. What characterizes it? Though there is one controlling principle for the function of a Baptist church, what qualities identify it as distinct from other Christian churches?

This chapter gives a summary of eight distinctives that Baptists have held with varying degrees of importance throughout their history. My purpose is to aid you in seeing Baptist beliefs by providing a simple list with minimal explanation.

We cannot turn to any authoritative listing of Baptist distinctives. Various Baptist writers have differing lists. Some include one basic distinctive with all the others subsidiary. Others list three, five or more. But all Baptists will essentially agree that the distinctives listed here are expressive of our position, even though they may not list all of them separately.

We call these distinctive beliefs of Baptist churches. On the other hand, we are aware that other churches and denominations hold firmly to some of these tenets as well.

These distinctives are formulated differently from a

statement of faith, although most of these distinctives will be included or implied in an affirmation of faith. Many individual churches have their own statements of faith, and most denominations have some kind of statement of faith even though the denomination is non-creedal in its basic position. Statements of faith are doctrinal in nature. Baptists believe in all of the great doctrines of the Christian faith as enunciated in the historic creeds. The distinctives we are listing are not so much doctrinal as functional.

These eight statements of distinctives are only in summary fashion because all are dealt with more extensively throughout this book. Some may partially overlap.

1) *The New Testament is the sole and sufficient rule of faith and function.* We believe the entire Bible to be the inspired written revelation of God, but it is the New Testament that gives us the authority for faith and activity in the church. The Old Testament was prophetic of and preparatory to the new covenant, which is the period of the church. We believe our Lord fulfilled the old covenant and gave us the new to guide the life of the church now. This further indicates that we hold no creed or statement of faith as binding upon the church. We believe there are values in creeds and statements of faith as indications of our understanding of New Testament doctrine, but none of these can be authoritative for the faith and work of the church.

2) *It is the privilege of each individual to have direct access to God through Jesus Christ.* This is known as the universal priesthood of believers. The only priesthood we know in the New Testament is that of every believer in Jesus Christ. No human being or human agency can interfere with a soul's relationship to God. This further places all people on an equal plane before God. It removes distinctions between clergy and laity. This "direct access" idea underlies all the others that we hold dear as Baptists.

3) *The church and state are to be completely separate in*

their respective fields. The state is not to interfere with the distinctly religious functions of the church. It is to give complete liberty to all its citizens to worship according to the dictates of their consciences. The state is not to demand any particular religious belief for participation in government service, nor to refuse anyone participation in government activity because of a certain religious affiliation. The church is not to interfere with the functions of the state except as it might arouse public opinion about a violation of a biblical or moral issue. A true Baptist will strive to preserve this separation and real liberty for all human beings to worship as they desire.

4) *The church's government is a simple, democratic form.* A democratic church government is called the *congregational* form. This means each member in a Baptist church has as much authority as any other member, including the pastor. We are aware that pastors carry an authority in their leadership roles as those called of God and democratically elected by the people of the church, but in the actual voting on policies and decisions the pastor's vote is only as authoritative as any other member's. The same might be said of denominational leadership. Denominational leaders carry significant authority as leaders called of God and elected by the democratic process, but in voting privileges their votes count no more than any other delegate to district or national meetings. Each church also has its own independence and autonomy in local function, though each of these churches recognizes the necessary dependence on one another in a broader fellowship. Churches work with one another in a voluntary denominational affiliation for the sake of effective witness and service in the world.

5) *Baptism is for believers only and only by immersion.* The qualification for baptism is not a matter of age but of faith. Baptism follows trust in Christ. A subject for baptism must be old enough to understand the decision of faith in

Christ and must have made that decision before he or she is baptized. Only immersion constitutes New Testament baptism. It is only this form that properly fulfills the symbolism involved. No substitute form should ever be practiced, for it would violate the New Testament mode. Baptism does not save. If a person is not physically able to be baptized, he still may be saved. But baptism is necessary to full obedience to Christ unless one is providentially hindered.

6) *Church membership is for the regenerate only.* It is a concern of Baptist churches that only those who have had a genuine experience of faith in Christ should become church members. Anyone desiring to unite with a Baptist church must give evidence of personal faith in Christ. An unregenerate church membership soon leads to a weakened church with the possibility of ungodly practices. This was the condition of most churches in our country in the first half of the eighteenth century. It led to the necessity of the God-given Great Awakening in midcentury.

7) *Christ is the supreme Head of the church.* Jesus Christ must be Lord of the program and actions of each church. No group or individual can dominate the wishes of other members within a Baptist church. All are accountable to and under the direction of Christ. No action of the church should be contrary to His will. The late William Cleaver Wilkinson, a well-known Baptist in his day, wrote in a large book titled *The Baptist Principle,* "The true organizing principle of Baptist churches may be stated in three words: Obedience to Christ." This principle expresses the submission of believers to the supreme headship of Christ. Such obedience controls the glorious liberty that is ours as New Testament Christians.

8) *The evangelization of the world is our task.* Baptists take seriously the great commission (Matthew 28:19-20). Each member is responsible for the task of witnessing. The

remarkable growth of Baptist groups results from constant and varied evangelism endeavors. This emphasis also accounts for Baptists' strong emphasis on missions and distinguishes them as outstanding at recruiting young volunteers for Christian service.

These eight points sum up the distinct beliefs that make Baptists what they are. Church members should review them frequently in order to be familiar with them. These distinctives make for a rich heritage of which any Baptist may be proud. To understand these qualities is to make each of us desire to share these convictions with others, but willing to fight for the liberty of others to disagree.

5

Members:
A Unique Type of People

The character of any organization is determined largely by the character of the people in its constituency. You cannot separate the characteristics of any group from the character of those who make up the group. The strength of a building depends upon the materials and methods used in construction. Poorly laid footings will cause deterioration of the whole building.

The church is the Lord's building. The church is made up of people, and it is only as strong as the people who make up the membership. Conclusions about the church and its character are determined by conclusions about the lives of members.

It is evident that there were definite qualifications for church membership in the New Testament era. It is helpful to discover what these qualifications were. We can determine many from the use of the word *ecclesia*, discussed in chapter 2, which is translated "church" in the New Testament. Both in the Greek assembly and in the New Testament church organization, a person had to possess definite qualifications to be considered a member.

This truth is amplified by the very nature of the church

in the New Testament Scriptures. We would not want to add qualifications for church membership that are contrary to the New Testament, nor to omit anything that was definitely taught there.

A conversion experience

The first qualification is a conversion experience. One thing is crystal clear in the New Testament: those who were members of the church had a definite experience of faith in Christ. Their lives were different from the rest of the people outside the church.

Let's note a few examples from the New Testament. Speaking to Nicodemus, an important religious leader, the Lord Jesus said, "Unless a man is born again, he cannot see the kingdom of God" (John 3:3). This man who had been teaching many about religion and God had to learn the truth that a definite conversion experience was necessary for a person to know God. The new birth was the best way to describe this experience.

As I mentioned previously, the word Christian was a nickname not chosen by the Christians themselves. They were called "little Christs" because they were people whose lives were so different. They were Christlike. They did not get the name from the Jews, who would never call them Christians or little Messiahs. They did not take it themselves. It was given to them by the pagan people of Antioch who recognized that they lived like Christ and were different from all other people.

The word Christian is used only three times in the New Testament. In Acts 11:26 we read, "The disciples were first called Christians at Antioch." Again it is used in Acts 26:28 when King Agrippa said to Paul, "Do you think that in such a short time you can persuade me to be a Christian?" It is found the third time in 1 Peter 4:16 where Peter says,

"If you suffer as a Christian, do not be ashamed." These three passages clearly indicate three qualifications of early church Christians.

First, believers were *a distinct people.* Everywhere in the New Testament this was evident in the lives of those who trusted Christ—they stood out in contrast to those around them. The Lord Jesus said in John 15:19: "If you belonged to the world, it would love you as its own. As it is, you do not belong to the world, but I have chosen you out of the world. That is why the world hates you." Distinctness of life was a definite qualification.

Second, Christians had *a definite experience.* Something new and different had taken place in their lives. It was an experience they could express to others. The apostle Paul says in Ephesians 2:1-2: "As for you, you were dead in your transgressions and sins, in which you used to live when you followed the ways of this world and of the ruler of the kingdom of the air, the spirit who is now at work in those who are disobedient." The experience is as radical as a transformation from death to life.

Third, this new life had *a specific beginning.* Every person has a physical beginning. Every Christian has a spiritual beginning. No individual possesses this life at the time of his physical birth. The believer may not be able to name the time, but he must know that there was a beginning to his spiritual life. In Romans 6:20,22 we read: "When you were slaves to sin, you were free from the control of righ-teousness... But now that you have been set free from sin and have become slaves to God, the benefit you reap leads to holiness, and the result is eternal life." The Christian life has a specific beginning.

Now we might ask, "How did this new life begin?" or "How may one get it?" First, there must be *a recognition of need.* Unless a person realizes that he is lost without Christ there is no possibility of receiving new life or a conversion experience. In Romans 3:23 we read, "For all have sinned and fall short of the glory of God."

Second, a person must confess that need by *repenting of personal sin.* Salvation is an individual matter. Each person must face his or her own sin and need of the Lord. When some raised the thought that certain slaughtered Galileans were terrible sinners, Jesus said twice, "Unless you repent, you too will all perish" (Luke 13:3). It is easy to think of others as sinners and in need of repentance and not make it personal, but each one must face oneself in one's own relationship to God.

Third, one must *ask the Lord for forgiveness and cleansing.* In 1 John 1:9 we read, "If we confess our sins, he is faithful and just and will forgive us our sins and purify us from all unrighteousness." It is a beautiful experience to be forgiven and to have the burden of sin and guilt removed.

Fourth, *Jesus Christ must be received* into the life by faith. It is an amazing truth that He will live His life in us. That makes the beginning of the Christian life a new birth. In John 1:12-13 we read: "Yet to all who received him, to those who believed in his name, he gave the right to become children of God—children born not of natural descent, nor of human decision or a husband's will, but born of God."

Finally, *thanksgiving should be expressed* to the Lord for doing His saving work. To thank Him is an act of faith in believing that He has done what He promised. It is amazing what this does to the new convert. Sometimes it is difficult for a person to thank the Lord, but thanksgiving is a confirmation of the act of believing.

These steps, taken in genuine conviction and faith, will bring a person to new life.

Many groups think that non-Christians should be received into the membership of the church, so they can learn of Christ and put their trust in Him. State churches in Europe have followed this policy. This was also true in the churches in the early days of our country. Though people had come for religious freedom, church leaders demanded that everyone be a member of their church to be a citizen of the state. As a result many became members who did not know what it was to have a conversion experience. A church filled with unconverted people will soon deteriorate.

How can we speak of the church as the salt of the earth when it becomes so mixed with the world that it no longer flavors the world with its godly character? How can we speak of it as the light of the world when the world is a part of the church? A church member must have a conversion experience. This was true in the New Testament church, and it should be true in the modern church.

A confession of faith

Most people find it easy to talk about the events and issues of life. We especially like to talk about our exciting experiences. Why is it that we often are tongue-tied about our spiritual experience? An encounter with Christ is the most thrilling and most important experience a person can have. We believe that one of the qualifications for membership is a verbal expression of faith in Jesus Christ. How else can the church know whether the applicant has had a conversion experience?

Listen to the Word of God. Psalm 66:16 says: "Come and listen, all you who fear God; let me tell you what he has done for me." We also read in Psalm 107:2: "Let the redeemed of the Lord say this—those he redeemed from the hand of the foe." The Lord Jesus says in Mark 8:38: "If anyone is ashamed of me and my words in this adulterous and sinful generation, the Son of man will be ashamed of him when he comes in his Father's glory with the holy angels." Then again Paul says in Romans 10:9-10: "That if you confess with your mouth, 'Jesus is Lord,' and believe in your heart that God raised him from the dead, you will be saved. For it is with your heart that you believe and are justified, and it is with your mouth that you confess and are saved."

The Bible clearly emphasizes the need for confession of faith. Thus, a Baptist church expects everyone to give a confession of his faith in Jesus Christ. This expression may be given to the church as a group, or it may be given to a representative body, such as the deacon or elder board, which passes it on with a recommendation to the church as a whole.

There are understandable objections to this. Concerning their spiritual experience, some may say, "This is a private matter." We can appreciate this concern, but how can the church know if the person has had a conversion experience unless the applicant says he has put his trust in Jesus Christ? On a rare occasion someone may find it nearly impossible to audibly declare his faith to a group of people. It might then be arranged to have that person write out his or her testimony and have it read.

An external expression of faith

In the New Testament, people testified to their faith by being baptized. Baptism portrays an outward expression of the believer's inner experience. The way in which New Testament baptism is observed declares the glory of our life in Christ. One is immersed in the water to give indication of his or her identity with Jesus Christ. The believer is buried in water and raised again signifying that he or she has experienced a from-death-to-life conversion because Jesus died and was buried and raised again. It further indicates that the believer is living a new life. This burial in water symbolizes that the Christian is dead to the old life.

Many churches do not follow New Testament baptism. The New Testament method is immersion and is only for those who have put their faith in Jesus Christ. Sometimes Baptists are accused of making baptism the central issue of their churches. That is not true. Baptists are primarily concerned that every individual have a personal faith in the Lord Jesus. Such faith makes one a child of God. Baptism does not save. It does not change a life. Baptism follows faith and gives outward expression of something that has already taken place.

Those who were added to the fellowship were first baptized. Baptism became a badge of one's faith—putting on a uniform. When I entered the navy as a young man, I was inducted in Minneapolis, but I did not get my uniform until about three weeks later when I reached Boston. For three weeks I was as much in the Navy as any other man who might be sailing the high seas, but nobody could tell it because I did not have the uniform. Many people have put their trust in Jesus Christ, but have never given outward expression to it—and thus others do not know about their spiritual experience.

Baptism should signify cutting ties with the previous Christless life. Because immersion is such a graphic illustration of this separation, most denominations use this method of baptism on their overseas mission fields. Baptism signifies a real break with all pagan ties. In many countries nationals can easily claim to receive Christ and can become active in the work of the church without causing conflict. The real conflict comes at the time of their baptism. The willingness to be immersed becomes the test of the believer's sincerity. Such a step means a clear break with the old life.

The New Testament teaches, and the modern church ought to observe, that baptism is one qualification for church membership. Receiving Jesus Christ brings one into the fellowship of Christians. Being baptized *declares* one's fellowship with other believers. Church membership is a tangible expression of our membership in the universal church. These tangible expressions of our spiritual experience are crucial to our effective Christian walk.

A Christian life

At the beginning of this chapter I noted that the church is characterized by the lives of its members. This is one of the weak areas in church life today. Not only do we insist on a conversion experience, a confession of faith and an external expression of faith in baptism, we must see faith revealed in life. Paul said in 2 Corinthians 5:17: "Therefore, if any one is in Christ, he is a new creation; the old has gone, the new has come!" The New Testament Christian was marked by a life distinct from that of others about him. Certainly those in the modern church also ought to be marked by a distinct life because they belong to the Lord.

One source of weakness in the church is the unchristlike lives of its members. The strength of the church must be guarded by regularly emphasizing purity of life. If the church is too tolerant in the matter of Christian living, decay will go on until the church will no longer tolerate a ministry that preaches the complete gospel—the gospel that deals with sin.

For the church to be effective it must be pure, a fellowship of people who believe in living godly lives. Every Christian must discover personal responsibility to God, to oneself and to those who observe the Christian's life. Witness the experience of Joseph in Potiphar's house as told in Genesis 39. When he was tempted by Potiphar's wife to commit an immoral act, Joseph responded, "How then could I do such a wicked thing and sin against God?" He also felt a responsibility to Potiphar and others, as well as his own well-being. Consider also 1 Corinthians 5 and 8, as well as Colossians 3:1-2.

It is interesting to observe that people outside the church expect believers to exhibit godly lives. Again and again that expectation is expressed orally as well as in print.

In the developing nations, a new Christian is usually not allowed to become a church member until he has lived the Christian life through a trial period. When he proves by his changed life that he has had a genuine conversion experience, then he may unite with the church. During the Communist reign in Eastern Europe, a new convert needed witnesses to testify that he or she was a genuine Christian as confirmed by a changed lifestyle. Then that person was allowed to be baptized and unite with the church.

Obviously, we do not have the same circumstances confronting us. But we have the same gospel. We have the same Lord. We need transformed lives for church membership because that is New Testament Christianity.

Reception into the church

Once the four previously mentioned qualifications are met, a church votes on receiving the individual into its membership. Membership in the local church, as it is revealed in the New Testament, is voluntary on the part of both the individual and the church. The individual may or may not join according to his or her own conviction and decision. Likewise the church may or may not accept the one who desires to join.

Baptists believe that believers must be a part of the local church to fulfill the will of the Lord, but it is a voluntary matter because each believer must make the decision to do so. When the local church makes its decision, it does so on the basis of the qualifications that have been previously considered. If a person has given evidence of possessing these qualifications, then he or she will be received into the church.

A person who has been a member of one Baptist church usually may transfer to another Baptist church by letter. That is, the person is given a letter of transfer and recommendation in order that he might unite with another Baptist church. But many churches today expect a confession of faith even from those who unite by letter. This has become necessary because sometimes church members may not have had a genuine conversion experience.

Then again a person may unite by experience. This means the individual has been baptized according to the New Testament method, but is not a member of a Baptist church or any church. He comes on the basis of a confession of his faith in Christ.

The membership of the church is made up of those who have had a conversion experience, who give confession of faith, who give expression of their faith in baptism, and who are living a Christian life. Each candidate must be voted on by the church to be received into its local membership.

The local church is Christ's church. Even with its limitations and failures it is still His church. To be a part of it is a high privilege and a great responsibility.

6

Baptism: Showing Our Faith and Obedience

Ceremony is a part of human need and experience. Human beings create their own rites and ceremonies when they do not have any. The Lord who created us knows our yearnings, desires and needs. He made us this way. He knows what would be necessary for adequate spiritual function for us as human beings. For that reason He gave us simple but meaningful ceremonies that picture profound truths. In a very real sense these ceremonies become nonverbal sermons. No words need to be spoken. The rites themselves picture the truths.

The New Testament specifies two *ordinances* for the church: baptism and the Lord's Supper. Baptism is observed only once by an individual, while the Lord's Supper is observed repeatedly. In this chapter we will consider baptism, the initial ceremony in the life of a Christian. (I do not use the word in the sense of initiating a person into some society, though membership in the local church usually follows.)

Many churches use the term "sacrament" in place of ordinance. Most Baptists avoid the word "sacrament." We prefer "ordinance" because it signifies outward rites, "ordained" by the Lord Himself, to symbolize inner spiritual experiences.

For many people "sacrament" suggests that God does something to the individual who participates, apart from his or her own faith or spiritual understanding. The word "sacrament" is from the word *sacramentum*, signifying the oath taken by the Roman soldier to obey his commander even unto death. If the word still carried this meaning we would not object to its use today; for we believe that baptism and the Lord's Supper are sacraments in the sense that they are vows of allegiance to Christ our Lord.

When we turn to the New Testament, we find these two ordinances so simple in form and so expressive in meaning we would never desire to change them. They are not only visible signs; they are teaching opportunities that make more graphic our spiritual heritage in Christ.

The meaning of baptism

Most people know Baptists believe that immersion in water is the true method (mode) of baptism. Some ask, "Why doesn't the Bible say immerse if that is what baptism means?" That's exactly what it does say! The word baptism is not an English word. It is a Greek word Anglicized—it was transliterated from the Greek *baptizo*. Our English Bible, sometimes called the Authorized Version, was translated in England in 1611 under the direction of King James. The church was already practicing methods of baptism other than immersion. Thus, to avoid conflict, the scholars did not translate the word *baptizo*. They only made the Greek word into an English word.

In the early days of the Bible society movements this action caused a problem. Those who believed the word should be translated objected to the transliteration and formed their own Bible societies. They published and distributed their own translations of the Bible.

What do authorities on the Greek language say about the meaning of the word? Let's consider five well-known lexicons, Greek dictionaries. The classical Greek lexicon was written by Liddell and Scott (revised by Jones and McKenzie), Church of England men. The New Testament Greek lexicon was compiled by Thayer, a scholar of the Congregational Church. The lexicon of theological terms was written by a German Lutheran named Cremer. Bauer's Lexicon, translated by Arndt and Gingrich, is also Lutheran. The study in Kittel, Volume I, is by Oepke, another Lutheran. All these men agree that the word *baptizo* means *to dip, immerse, submerge or overwhelm.*

Thomas J. Conant in his *Meaning and Use of Baptizein* sums up a study of the use of the word throughout the history of Greek literature with these words: "In all the word has retained its ground meaning without change. From the earliest age of Greek literature down to its close, a period of about 2000 years, not an example has been found in which the word has any other meaning."

The words "sprinkling" or "pouring" are never used in the New Testament for baptism. This has compelled scholars of all denominations to admit that in the original meaning and in New Testament use baptism meant immersion. Martin Luther said: "The term *baptism* is a Greek word. It may be rendered *a dipping,* when we dip something in water, that it may be entirely covered with water." Another Protestant Reformer, John Calvin, says: "The word 'baptize' signifies to *immerse;* and the rite of immersion was observed by the ancient church." Brenner, a Roman Catholic, says, "For 1300 years was baptism generally and regularly an immersion of the person under water, and only in extraordinary cases, a sprinkling or pouring with water. The latter was moreover disputed as a mode of baptism, nay even forbidden." Other theologians could be mentioned, but this is sufficient to show us the wide acceptance of the meaning of the word baptism.

We then ask, "How and when did sprinkling become the method of baptism?" This mode arose because people came to feel there was something magical about baptism— that it brought salvation to the recipient. This concept cannot be supported by Scripture, but if that were your belief, a person dying before being baptized would be lost. A sick or injured person could not be immersed because of his physical condition, but if baptism were necessary to salvation, he would be eternally lost if he should die. Thus, sprinkling began to be practiced.

The first instances of sprinkling appear to have occurred in the third century A.D., but it was done only occasionally until the fourteenth century when the option of sprinkling *or* immersion became officially adopted. Not until 1644 did the Church of England adopt sprinkling by vote of Parliament. The year before it had been voted on and recommended to Parliament by the Assembly of Divines. The vote was 25 to 24 in favor of sprinkling.

Before we leave the meaning of the word baptism, we must also consider those who believe water baptism is not for this age. This is the position of a few liberals who have departed from many basic principles of the gospel, and do not accept the New Testament as the authoritative guide for church activity. But it is also the position of some who accept the authority of the New Testament. These believe that the only essential baptism now is the baptism of the Holy Spirit. They follow the teachings of E.W. Bullinger of another day. Bullinger put forth a system of Bible study that breaks up the unity of the Word of God. This system is completely unwarranted.

In view of these various opinions about the word, it will be helpful for us to consider a study of the use of "baptism" in the New Testament. The word is found 99 times in its various forms, excluding its use as part of the proper name, John the Baptist. Sometimes the word is found several times in one or two verses. These are all counted. Fifteen times it is used in a figurative sense. Fourteen of these times refer to Christ's sufferings when He would be *overwhelmed by the suffering* of bearing the sins of the world upon the cross. The other one refers to Israel crossing the Red Sea under the leadership of Moses. Seven times it refers to the *baptism of the Holy Spirit,* and four of these times it refers to Christ baptizing with the Holy Spirit. That leaves 77 times when the word refers to *water baptism.* Only three of these could be considered even by strained interpretation to be Spirit baptism.

Thus, a good principle to follow is: The Scriptures are speaking of water baptism unless baptism by the Holy Spirit is clearly indicated.

The symbolism of baptism

Ordinances are outward symbols of inner spiritual experience. Baptism portrays the beginning of the Christian's spiritual life. How? Read Romans 6:1-10 and Colossians 2:12. First, *baptism pictures the believer's identification with Jesus Christ,* who was crucified, buried and raised again for his salvation. Salvation is the result of what Christ accomplished by His death. Baptism expresses symbolically and publicly what has taken place in the transformed life, and it further expresses a new allegiance to Christ. At one time the individual was devoted to the world and its activities. Now Christ is the object of his loyalty.

In 1 Corinthians 10:2 we read: "They were all baptized into Moses in the cloud and in the sea." This illustrates what we are saying about identification and allegiance. Baptism is an expression of allegiance to a lord. In this illustration the people of Israel were committed to Moses, their lord. That is true in the baptism of the Christian in his allegiance to Jesus Christ. Because baptism is a graphic expression of allegiance, almost all denominations use immersion in their overseas work.

Second, *baptism symbolizes the new life of the believer.* The believer must consider himself dead to sin. Baptism graphically portrays this experience as the believer is buried in water and raised again. He is buried to the old life and raised to new life, which is already a spiritual experience for him. In 2 Corinthians 5:17 we read: "Therefore, if anyone is in Christ, he is a new creation; the old has gone, the new has come!" Read also Galatians 2:20. Physical burial breaks the last tie a person has with this life. The same thing is true in the spiritual life. When a person becomes a Christian, by faith he is dead and buried to the present life of sin and alive to new life in Christ. He has a completely new set of values for life. No other form of baptism could give the picture of this experience.

Third, *baptism portrays the believer's glorification.* There is a forward look involved in this symbol. The resurrection day is coming, and baptism says expressively that we believe in the reality of this resurrection. Death is the last enemy of life, but it has been conquered by Christ in His resurrection. By faith in Him we too may conquer death and participate in the resurrection. Read 1 Corinthians 15:26, 55-57. Burial in water is the only proper method by which to portray these truths.

The significance of baptism's symbolism is illustrated by the experience of a man in a church I pastored. This man loved the Lord. Though active in our church, he was not a member when I came. He belonged to a church of another denomination which proclaimed the gospel but did not insist on immersion for baptism. In his infancy he had been sprinkled. Along with others in that church he began a serious study of Scripture after he trusted Christ as Savior.

From this study he came to believe that baptism should follow faith in Christ.

One summer a group from that church went down to a river and were baptized. This man and his wife intended to be baptized, but her physical condition prevented them. Some time went by, and this couple still desired to give testimony of their faith in Christ by baptism. They reasoned that the amount of water did not make any difference, so they were baptized by sprinkling a second time as a testimony of their faith in Christ.

Then they moved to our area and became very active in the work of our church. They could not become members because they had not been baptized by immersion. They experienced a real spiritual struggle over this problem. Finally, in studying and praying about it, they recognized they had not fulfilled the significant symbolism involved in baptism, and were baptized by immersion.

The candidates for baptism

By "candidates" for baptism I mean those who qualify for baptism. Some say Baptists believe in adult baptism only. This is not true because we baptize some children. A child who is old enough to understand the gospel and believe in Christ may be baptized. Caution is in order, however. The child must be old enough to clearly understand and voluntarily choose to be baptized. The New Testament principle is that a person must be a believer before baptism takes place. Read the texts in the New Testament that have to do with baptism. Here are some of them: Acts 2:41; 8:12-13,36-37; 9:18.

Do these qualifications do away with the baptism of infants? They certainly do. There is no infant baptism in the New Testament. Some have attempted to use scriptural mention of what is termed "household baptism" as evidence for infant baptism. "Household baptism" is mentioned five times: 1) Cornelius in Acts 10:47-48; 2) Lydia in Acts 16:15; 3) the Philippian jailer in Acts 16:31-33; 4) Crispus in Acts 18:8, and 5) Stephanas in 1 Corinthians 1:16. An examination of these texts and their contexts reveals that nothing is said about infants or even children. We do not even know for certain that Lydia was married. The household of that day included all who lived in the home, even servants. A study of these passages in full context indicates that faith in Christ was a prerequisite for each person in the household.

The Roman Catholic Church sprinkles infants as its method of baptism. Yet Archbishop Hughes, a Roman Catholic, says: "It does not appear from Scripture that even one infant was ever baptized; therefore, Protestants should reject infant baptism on their own principles, that the Scriptures are their only rule of faith and practice, and that infant baptism has an unscriptural usage." The Roman Catholic Church can be consistent in its use of sprinkling for baptism only because it considers its own tradition to be authoritative for its actions.

Texts often used to support infant baptism are Matthew 18:1-10 and 19:13-15, where Jesus blesses the children. Nothing is said in these places about either baptism or salvation. These passages do not even indicate that the children were infants. Had the Lord been teaching baptism of little ones, the apostles would never have rebuked their parents for bringing them. If this had anything to do with salvation, the apostles would have been glad to welcome the parents and children.

Faith in Christ must *precede* baptism. If baptism is essential for salvation, then the will of another person in addition to the will of the sinner and of God must be obtained. This is seriously in conflict with the New Testament doctrine of salvation.

A further question about baptism: What about repeating the ceremony? Briefly, it may be repeated only if the symbol was not actually picturing the condition of the individual the first time. In other words, if the individual was not really a child of God the first time, then the outward act may be repeated.

The obligation to be baptized

Since salvation is by faith and faith alone, some people believe that baptism is not essential. Did Christ ever give a command that was nonessential? A young man asked a student for the ministry, "Why do you Baptists insist so strenuously upon a ceremony which saves no one?"

The student answered, "If it were a condition of salvation would you do it the Baptists' way?

"Instantly," replied the fellow.

"Then," the student answered, "this seems to be your position: to serve your own interests you will obey God, but not for the sake of Christ who commanded this act."

If it means nothing, why do it in any form? If it means anything, why not use the right form?

Read the great commission that our Lord gave in Matthew 28:19-20. Is there any indication that it has been canceled? If it has not, then we are commissioned to baptize those who have believed. Read Acts 2:38. Many under conviction after Peter's Pentecostal sermon asked what they should do. Peter's reply included both repentance and baptism. Read Paul's testimony in Acts 22:16. To the apostle, baptism was an obligation.

The Lord Jesus not only commanded baptism, but observed it Himself (Matthew 3:13-17). It certainly was not essential for Him, because John's baptism was a baptism for repentance. Jesus did not need to repent because He never sinned, but He identified Himself with sinning mankind that needed repentance. This act also prefigured His death, burial and resurrection. If He was willing, though it was nonessential, shouldn't we be willing?

7

The Lord's Supper: A Death to Remember

The value of ceremony is to crystallize truths and ideas through tangible pictures. Some of these rites are one-time events. Others are repeated events. The recurring events are necessary to prevent us from forgetting or neglecting significant truths for effective living. That is the reason for the recurring ceremony of the Lord's Supper, given by our Lord.

In the preceding chapter we noticed that there are only two ordinances in the New Testament: baptism and the Lord's Supper. Both refer to the death of Christ, but each expresses a different aspect of how His death affects Christians. Baptism indicates that *we are in Christ* as a result of His death, while the Lord's Supper shows that *Christ is in us* because of His death.

Baptism symbolizes the beginning of the Christian life and the Lord's Supper the continuance of the Christian life. Baptism portrays regeneration, while the Lord's Supper pictures sanctification or the growth of the believer in holy living. Baptism testifies to the new birth of the child of God and the Lord's Supper to his development. Baptism is a witness to Christ's cleansing power and the Lord's Supper to His sustaining power. As we observe these relationships, the ordinances become more significant in our thinking.

In this chapter we consider the Lord's Supper, the recurring ordinance of the church. This ceremony is one of the most graphic acts of worship that we can experience. It is accompanied by a solemnity, dignity and sacredness seldom experienced in any other act of worship. It is also a joyous celebration.

The meaning of the Lord's Supper

In the New Testament we find fewer references to the Lord's Supper than to baptism. This may surprise some people. The only places that distinctly refer to the Lord's Supper are once each in Matthew, Mark and Luke and in 1 Corinthians 10 and 11.

In John 6 Jesus says He is the bread of life. He adds that it is necessary to eat His flesh and drink His blood to have life, but this is not a direct reference to the Lord's Supper. In Acts 2:42, 46 we find the disciples breaking bread in fellowship with one another. This may refer to receiving the Lord's Supper, but this is not necessarily so. The expression "They broke bread in their homes and ate together..." may merely express a beautiful bond of fellowship. Acts 20:7 records that the disciples broke bread on the first day of the week. This may have been the Lord's Supper, but again we cannot be certain of this. These are the only references to weekly bread-breaking that we find in the New Testament.

That the references are few does not minimize the significance of the ordinance. It was established by the Lord. He specifically said, "Do this in remembrance of me." Christians continued to observe it throughout the early history of the church. It made sacred the fellowship of believers with the Lord and with one another.

The Lord's Supper was established the evening before Christ's death, during Jesus' and the disciples' observance of the Jewish Passover feast. The Lord's Supper supersedes the Passover feast. Now we observe His feast and will continue to do so "until he comes." When He does come, this communion will be superseded by the marriage feast of the Lamb.

The Passover looked back to a glorious day of deliverance from slavery in Egypt, and it looked forward to the coming of the true Prophet of God to deliver His people permanently. *The Lord's Supper* looks back to our deliverance from the slavery of sin through the death of Christ on the cross, and it looks forward to the coming of the victorious King as conqueror of sin, evil and the world. When Christ comes, *the marriage feast of the Lamb* will cause us to look back to our deliverance from this world and this body of sin and will give us a forward look to an endless eternity of fellowship with the Lord of Glory.

How significant is this ordinance when we recognize its place in the total plan of God!

Now consider the elements used in the Lord's Supper—the bread and the wine. Each is important as a symbol of the Lord's work for us. Broken bread portrays the body of the Lord Jesus, which was broken so that we might be made whole. The cup of grape juice or wine reminds us of His blood shed for our sins. He who lived without sinning bore our sin. This was necessary, for "without the shedding of blood there is no forgiveness."

As we participate in the fellowship of the Lord's Supper, He gives blessing in answer to our obedience and faith. However, we do not believe the ordinance is sacramental; that is, we do not believe that mere participation will bring the grace of the Lord. In the light of this belief we must understand the viewpoints of other groups.

The Roman Catholic Church holds a view different

from ours. It believes in "transubstantiation," which means that the bread and wine are actually changed into the body and blood of Christ when consecrated (made holy through prayer) by the priest. We are not able to accept that position for several reasons. First, this view suggests a repetition of Christ's sacrifice. A Catholic study book says in relation to the changed bread and wine: "So that his sacrifice might for ever be renewed and re-lived in his church he gave to men the power to do as he had done. It is at mass each day in all parts of the world that this offering of Christ is renewed." (Read in this regard Hebrews 10:12.) Second, it is contrary to the evidence of the human senses. Scientists can easily show that the elements do not actually change to flesh and blood and human taste reveals the same thing. Third, it also makes illogical our Lord's statement when He established the Lord's Supper. He said, "This is my body ... This is my blood." When He said it, He was sitting in the midst of the apostles. No one reading the text can sensibly believe He meant that the elements actually turned into His flesh and blood (John 6:63).

Christ made other statements in the same vein. He said on one occasion, "I am the door." He said, "I am the way" and "I am the vine." No one takes these to mean that He suddenly changed into a door or a vine or some roadway. Nor do His upper room statements indicate that the bread and wine change to be His flesh and blood. We must understand such statements in the context in which they were spoken.

Other positions are a carryover of only a partial return to scriptural doctrine during the Reformation. Lutherans hold a position sometimes described as "consubstantiation." By this they mean that the bread and wine do not actually change to the body and blood of Christ, but His body and blood are present "in and with and under" when a believer partakes of the elements. That is a modification of Roman Catholic doctrine.

Presbyterians and some other Protestants believe in the mystical presence of the Lord in the supper. John Calvin said, "All are truly made partakers of the proper substance of the body and blood of Christ." That view goes beyond a symbolic belief in the ordinance; it makes the Lord present in a spiritual way because of the presence of the Lord's Supper. However, the Lord is present *wherever* His own are gathered together. Though we speak of the Lord's Supper as symbolical, that does not minimize its high significance. We obediently receive it regularly because our Lord instituted it. The special blessing of Christ's presence becomes ours because we are acting by faith in Him. The grace of God is not given merely through the elements taken, but by our faith relationship to Christ represented by the elements in the supper.

The supper, repeatedly received, symbolically expresses our need to feed continually upon the Lord. We maintain our Christian experience and grow in our Christian life as we depend on the Lord. Just as we eat and drink to sustain our physical life so we need daily to abide in the Lord for spiritual growth. That is the reason this is a recurring ordinance in Baptist churches.

The symbolism of the Lord's Supper

The Lord's Supper represents remembrance, fellowship, proclamation and a covenant.

First, this sacred rite is *a remembrance* of something Christ has accomplished for us. Jesus said, "Do this in remembrance of me." All of us have pictures or photos that bring to mind the joys of former fellowship. The Lord's Supper is a pictorial way of reminding us of the great blessings our Lord has accomplished for us.

We learn much from sermons. We come to appreciate pictures of Christ in children's Bibles, even though no one actually knows what our Lord looked like when He lived on earth. We read the Bible and receive a word from the Lord that constantly gives blessing. With all of this there is still more that we need—and that is found in receiving the Lord's Supper. Nothing can take its place in worship. In a nonverbal way it reminds us of the significance of Christ's death for us.

The Lord's Supper also portrays *a fellowship.* This communion involves a fellowship with the Lord as well as a fellowship among believers (1 Corinthians 10:16-17). When we eat the broken bread and drink the fruit of the vine, we express the vital relationship to the Lord that we have already experienced. He dwells in us by His Spirit. It is a communion so intimate that words cannot describe it, but the Lord's Supper can picture it.

Such fellowship demands utter loyalty to Jesus Christ. There can be no communion between opposing forces. It is impossible for a person to be loyal to the world and loyal also to Jesus Christ. As we participate in the Lord's Supper, we express our complete loyalty to Him.

An additional aspect of fellowship is the believer-with-believer relationship. The text says, "We, who are many, are one body." Ill will between believers receiving the Lord's Supper is an utter violation of this sacred communion. Such sin must be judged, confessed and righted, or God will judge the sinning persons. The fellowship at the Lord's Supper should make us particularly conscious of our bond with fellow believers. It makes us keenly aware that we are one body so that the love of believer for believer far exceeds normal human friendships.

The Lord's Supper is also *a proclamation* of our Lord. It is proclaiming or preaching the death of our Lord until He returns. The apostle Paul said, "For whenever you eat this bread and drink this cup, you proclaim the Lord's death until he comes." Sincere participation becomes a genuine testimony to unbelievers who observe our participation in it. For this reason many pastors invite everyone to remain in the sanctuary as the Lord's Supper is received. Though they are asked not to participate, unbelievers are invited to remain, observing an object lesson of the work of the Lord for sinners.

One well-known pastor serving in a university town said that more students were reached for Jesus Christ through witnessing the Lord's Supper than through almost any other means in the work of his church. This ordinance is real preaching if we trust the Lord to use it that way.

Also the Lord's Supper symbolizes *a covenant.* Our Lord said, "This...is the new covenant." That is where we get the names for the two parts of our Bible—the Old Testament and the New Testament represent the old covenant and the new covenant. The old covenant was expressed in the Passover feast, and now the new covenant between the believer and the Lord is pictured in the Lord's Supper.

Thus receiving the Lord's Supper indicates a binding covenant between the believer and his Lord. This covenant has a greater bond than any other kind of covenant or will that can be made. No will is actually effective until the death of the testator or the one involved in the covenant. Jesus died and shed His blood in order to seal the covenant between the believer and Himself. Thus, when we participate in the Lord's Supper, we are reminded of this binding covenant. Christ will never break His part of the covenant; we ought not break our part.

While this ordinance is a present obligation, it looks forward to another day. We observe the rite "until he comes." He may come at any time. Every time we participate in the communion we are reminded of His coming again. We would say with John, "Amen. Come, Lord Jesus!"

When we speak of the Lord's Supper as a symbol, don't conclude that what it suggests is unimportant. The Lord's Supper is highly significant. The Lord gave it for us to receive. We cannot omit it. It is part of our Christian experience.

Participants in the Lord's Supper

When we reflect on the meaning and significance of the Lord's Supper, we cannot help but know who is eligible to participate. An unbelieving person can hardly be a candidate for receiving the communion elements, which represent the broken body and shed blood of Jesus for our brokenness and sin. Only those who have believed Jesus' death was for their sake and have received Him into their lives should participate. In other words, the primary prerequisite to participation in the Lord's Supper is a genuine experience of faith in Christ.

A further requirement is an orderly, commendable Christian lifestyle. Instruction and care must be given for people to judge their worthiness to participate. Some sensitive people will find it difficult ever to take the elements because they never feel worthy. Others will treat the ceremony in a cavalier manner as just another event in the life of the church. They will not take seriously a concern for a godly lifestyle. Because of such difficulty in determining who should share in the supper, Paul wrote to the Corinthian church giving helpful instructions.

The believer is required to judge himself before participating in the communion (1 Corinthians 11:27-32). Believers must not participate "unworthily." Let us be clear on this. This does not mean that any of us are worthy or could be worthy in and of ourselves to take part in the Lord's Supper. It means that we must not partake in an unworthy manner. We must understand the significance of the ordinance in relation to Christ's death. He died for our sins. His body was broken. His blood was shed so we might be made whole and have forgiveness. Sin demands confession. We cannot share in the ceremony with unconfessed sin in our lives and have the blessing of the Lord. Paul wrote that some even died as a result of observing the ordinance without judging their own sin. This is serious. On the other hand, we must help the sensitive individual who may never feel he is worthy to partake. A participant in the Lord's Supper must be a believer in Jesus Christ, seeking to live a godly life. As individuals and as members of the body of Christ, we must be sure this truth is always recognized in our communion services.

Some churches permit only those who are baptized members of their church or denomination to participate in the Lord's Supper. There are varied reasons for those requirements. The communion service is a church ordinance. It usually is conducted in a local church. Further, baptism is a one-time event symbolizing the beginning of the Christian life; the Lord's Supper represents the continuation of the Christian life. One must have the beginning of life before one can continue that life. It is logical to have the ordinance that represents regeneration precede the one that represents growth.

Most churches now observe what we call "open communion" with certain definite limitations. These churches believe that all who know Jesus Christ as Savior and are seeking to live for Him should be permitted to participate. There are a number of reasons for this position. In the first place there is no clear indication in the New Testament that baptism is a prerequisite for participating in the Lord's Supper. Probably all who participated in the Lord's Supper in the early church were baptized, yet nothing is said about such a requirement.

Second, the Lord's Supper is the *Lord's* table. If He has

invited one to Himself in salvation, is it possible for any of us to restrict that saved person from the table of the Lord even though he is not baptized? It could be that the individual has not been taught about the New Testament method of baptism. It is possible that he is not physically able to be baptized. Yet that person is still a child of the Lord. Such a believer should have the right to observe the Lord's Supper.

In the third place, the Lord's Supper is a symbol. To us ordinances are symbolic expressions of spiritual experience. The ideal order is for baptism to precede participation in the Lord's Supper, but one symbol can hardly be a prerequisite for another symbol if the real experience of the Christian life is possessed by the participant.

In the fourth place, closed communion would violate one of the basic principles of the Baptist faith, the right of each individual to deal directly with the Lord. Although it is the right of the local church to guard its membership in order to maintain its standard and to require baptism by immersion before membership is permitted, yet participation in the Lord's Supper is the responsibility of the individual once the requirements of salvation and an orderly Christian life are made plain.

Some fear that open communion will lead to open membership, that persons not baptized by immersion would be permitted membership in the local church. To remove this fear we must remind ourselves of the purpose of the local church, which is fellowship, instruction and service. To be effective in these areas the membership will be composed of obedient believers. One of our Lord's clear commands is baptism for each believer. The church that compromises at this point will weaken its service and witness. The obedient believer will participate in both ordinances and be eligible for membership in the fellowship of the local church.

Robert Hall, a great Baptist leader in England in the last century, wrote about open communion: "The church desiring to avoid any misconception as to its distinctive position confines its membership to Baptists, but, seeing that the table is the Lord's, it argues that it is not for us as His disciples to exclude from it any who by faith have made themselves His." The ideal order is baptism first, but there is no evidence that it should be a prerequisite to receiving the Lord's Supper.

The obligation to share in the Lord's Supper

Since communion was an accepted practice of the early church, it is understandable that a specific command by the apostles was not necessary. Yet our Lord said to His apostles, "Do this in remembrance of me." This may not appear to be an urgent appeal to participate in the ordinance, but it indicates an obligation of love. How can we help but comply with somthing which graphically reminds us of His love for us? Would any of us think of destroying pictures of loved ones who have died? No. Yet, in a way, some of us are destroying the picture of the Lord in neglecting the Lord's Supper.

How often should the Lord's Supper be received? Most of our Baptist churches conduct it once a month. But Scripture gives no guidelines about its frequency. In Acts 2 we read of people breaking bread daily, though we are not certain that this referred to the Lord's Supper. If it was the communion supper, there is no indication that the Lord commanded such frequency.

Some believe that the Lord's Supper should be received every day when worship is conducted. This belief is based on Acts 2:46, which probably refers to the Lord's Supper, though we cannot be certain. Neither does the text say explicitly that believers observed the ceremony every week. They may have, but it was not obligatory. The New Testament gives no definite indication of what should be the frequency of participation.

It is always easy to hold the opinion, through prejudice, that the way we do anything is the best. Yet, most Baptists feel that once a month is the best arrangement for partaking the Lord's Supper. This is often enough not to neglect it, yet not so frequent as to lose its significance by familiarity.

The Lord's Supper is a solemn and sacred event, yet it is festal in nature. It stimulates our thoughts about our inner joy. It reminds us that our Lord drank the cup of suffering so we might drink the cup of joy. He drank the cup of condemnation so we might drink the cup of liberation. He drank the cup of death so we might drink the cup of life. How can we neglect such an ordinance when it reminds us of our rich heritage in Christ? And how can we help but receive it with celebration when we consider its powerful meaning to us?

8

Who Leads and Makes Decisions?

God is a God of order. Order is crucial to the effective functioning of our universe. This is true as well for individual human activity. Lack of order leads to chaos. Chaos in turn leads to anarchy, restricted freedom, ineffectiveness and destruction. Order is necessary to the successful activity of any institution or organization.

The Lord intended that the church function in an orderly manner. That began early in the life of the church. By the time of Acts 6 there was clear recognition that an embryonic organizational pattern was necessary to carry out the responsibilities of the church. Further development of that plan may be observed through the book of Acts. In concluding his discussion on the use of spiritual gifts, the apostle Paul says: "But everything should be done in a fitting and orderly way" (1 Corinthians. 14:40). For the church to be effective and function in an orderly manner, an organizational form is necessary.

For the ordinances of baptism and the Lord's Supper the New Testament provides explicit information to guide us. However, as we discuss the organization of the church we have no direct commands from the Lord. The New

Testament is our rule of faith. From its principles we must determine what should be the organization of the church—though it does not give explicit commands. The organization of our churches is important and must be under the leadership of the head of the church, the Lord Jesus.

The local church receives significant emphasis in the New Testament. Wherever believers are found in one locality, they band together for worship and Christian fellowship. This process has continued through the ages and in every land. Such groups could not maintain themselves without some form of organization. This is evident in the New Testament. As groups developed, it was necessary to form some organizational plan to maintain order and progress. Organization is also necessary to satisfy the human instinct for fellowship, the demand for harmonious activity, the need for Christian growth and for service.

The general positions

Five church positions are mentioned in the New Testament. Three of these are what we call the general offices of the church. These are not connected with a specific local church, but have a function that is related to all of the churches. Persons in these positions are usually itinerant servants. They travel from place to place in their service for Christ. Two of these positions do not exist today in the same sense they did in New Testament times. These two positions are those of the apostle and the prophet.

The title *apostle* was used in three ways in the New Testament. It referred to the twelve chosen by the Lord to be His immediate followers. It referred also to a larger body that included men like Paul and Barnabas. And it referred to some who were called "messengers" or "representatives" of the church (2 Corinthians 8:23; Philippians 2:25).

Apostles needed particular qualifications to hold this office. They were to give personal testimony to the fact of the Lord's resurrection. They must also have a special call and mission to perform, given by the Lord Himself. These two qualifications must be accompanied by signs or supernatural gifts to prove their apostleship. The work of the apostle was to set up the gospel program on earth. When the inauguration of the movement was complete, the position automatically ceased. Some of the apostles served in writing the New Testament. Some apostles were also called prophets. In several instances the two names are used for the same person.

Prophets were endowed with supernatural power for discerning the redemptive purposes of God, both future events and present spiritual relationships (Acts 11:27; 13:1; 15:32; 21:10, etc.). Some of these prophets, along with the apostles, gave us the New Testament. The essential task of the prophets was not to foretell the future, though that may have been part of their ministry. Their essential task was to proclaim God's message, that is, to be "forthtellers."

That task of the prophets is still being carried on. While they may not have quite the same function as the New Testament prophet, preachers of the Word of God are God's prophets today. The responsibility of predicting future events is cared for by the Bible so that the prophet need not function in that sense today.

The third general position is that of *evangelists*. The word is found only three times in the New Testament (Acts 21:8; Ephesians 4:11; 2 Timothy 4:5). The work of evangelists has continued through the ages to the present. Their responsibility is to enter new areas to extend the work of the church. They bring the good news of salvation to the unreached. They prepare the way for the pastors and teachers who are to follow up their work. Theirs is a pioneering task, moving into areas as yet untouched. For this reason many of our world missionaries are called evangelistic missionaries because they are entering unreached territories for Jesus Christ.

These are the general positions, because those who hold them do not remain with one local church.

The local positions

Those who hold the two other positions mentioned in the New Testament work with the local church. They are the *pastor* and the *deacon.* The word pastor is found only once in the English New Testament, but the same Greek word is used 17 other times where it is translated shepherd. There are other words used for the same office as pastor. These are bishop and elder. The word bishop is found only five times in the New Testament, and the word elder ten times.

"Bishop," "elder" and "pastor" are used interchangeably within the New Testament, though the different titles may suggest varied functions for the position. The term elder refers in most cases to the dignity of the position, while bishop or overseer, as it sometimes is translated, refers to the duties of the position. The word pastor refers to the tender care of a shepherd for the flock.

Notice how these words are used interchangeably by reading Acts 20:17 and 28. In the first instance the word elders is used, and in the second case the same persons are called overseers. Then turn to Titus 1:5, 7 and you find the same relationship for the two titles. We conclude from a study of the New Testament that the various duties and responsibilities of the bishop, elder, overseer and pastor describe the same position.

As one studies these various responsibilities and titles, one discovers that there are three general areas of duty. One is the preaching and teaching of the Word of God, which may be considered the most important responsibility. Compare Titus 1:9 and 2 Timothy 4:1-5. There is also the responsibility for the administration of the church. Read 1 Thessalonians 5:12-13. Third, there is the shepherding task encompassing the care of the members of the flock. See Acts 20:28 and Hebrews 13:17.

In the New Testament it appears that there was a plurality of elders in each church. There may be several reasons for this. In certain centers the church grew rapidly. That demanded several qualified leaders to keep the church functioning effectively. It is also possible that the growth of the church exceeded available facilities to accommodate the believers. That led to the use of house churches, which necessitated a plurality of leaders to serve these local groups.

We see that the terms pastor, overseer or bishop and elder are used interchangeably. The roles that are indicated in the New Testament suggest wide ranging responsibilities that must be fulfilled in the life of the church. It also makes clear the qualities a person must possess to fulfill this office. These qualities are delineated in 1 Timothy 3:1-7. They involve family relationships, his personal habits, motives and ambitions. It cannot be emphasized enough that the elder's character must be above reproach as much as is possible by the grace of God.

Before we proceed further in the organization of the church, we must look at the other position in the local church—the *deacon.* The New Testament refers to this position only a few times, but the word in the original language is used many times. Twenty times it is translated servant and seven times minister, which has the same meaning. First Timothy 3:8-13 lists the qualifications in some detail. They are similar to those of the pastor or elder and relate to the way the one runs one's household and family as well as one's personal life, motives and attitudes toward the work of the Lord.

The duties of a deacon may be observed in Acts 6, when they were first appointed. These seven men are not called deacons here, but it is accepted that they were the first deacons. They were appointed to provide for the temporal, secular and social needs of the church. They were responsible for the widows who needed care. The apostles could not fulfill this task because of their responsibilities of prayer, study and preaching.

In Philippians 1:1 deacons are addressed as a distinct group of workers, implying their spiritual responsibilities. A deacon is not merely chosen to serve the Lord's Supper. That is incidental to the task.

Deacon means servant. This word was also used to describe the apostles and even Christ. Those chosen to be deacons are servants of the church. This is the only thing that justifies their choice. No deacon or elder board can become dictatorial over the activities of the church and remain true to its high calling of serving. Our Lord was a servant. He declared to the apostles that they must serve if they wished to lead. The highest calling a person might have is to be a servant for the Lord's sake.

Some churches ordain deacons. This has New Testament precedent. In fact, there may be more evidence for the ordaining of deacons than there is for the ordaining of pastors or elders. In Acts 6 a body of disciples laid their hands upon seven men who were "known to be full of the Spirit and of wisdom" and prayed for them, setting them apart to the task—to "wait on tables" so that the disciples could "give [their] attention to prayer and the ministry of the word."

As we consider the position of deacon, it is natural to wonder about deaconesses. Only one text in the New Testament uses that designation. It is Romans 16:1, where Phoebe is spoken of as a servant. It is the very same word as deacon and can be translated either as deacon or deaconess.

This term referred to no specific official capacity within the church. It was not any certain elected or appointed office. Other women (and men) were serving similarly in the church. In 1 Timothy 5 we read of widows who were set apart to work in the church, but there is no indication that they held a specific office.

All of this very naturally raises the question of other present-day positions for the men and women of the church, such as Christian education workers, financial secretaries, etc. None other is mentioned in the New Testament, but we believe it is within the scope of the Scriptures that we have other positions. As churches grow, more workers are needed to administer the church activities efficiently. This is in accord with New Testament principles, because in the very beginning the church did not have deacons. They were appointed later to fulfill responsibilities that arose during New Testament times.

In our day most states and provinces demand that churches designate persons to care for the legal proceedings of the church. Many churches have *trustees* who are charged with the responsibility of their temporal affairs. Churches also need a treasurer and a clerk and a number of other officers to do the tasks that must be done within the church of Jesus Christ. It is conceivable that these functions could all be carried out by the deacons. That was probably done in the earlier days of the development of the church. Some churches today divide the deacon board into various groups to assume these responsibilities.

The government of the church

The form of government under which a church operates is significant. It makes a great difference in its function. Forms of government are extremely varied within the churches around the world. I will mention four types which seem to represent the major categories used by the different churches that claim to be Christian.

The first is the *collegial* form represented by the Roman Catholic Church and in part by the Greek Orthodox Church. The authority in the collegial form of government resides with the Pope and the bishops. All decisions that involve doctrine and methodology within the church are determined by the college of bishops guided by the action of synods and councils.

A second and similar form is the *episcopal* type of government, which is found in the Church of England and its counterpart in this country, the Episcopal Church, as well as the Methodist Church. Here the authority for the church resides in the general conference, composed of the bishops. For example, the local church does not appoint its own pastor. This is done by the area superintendent under the direction of the general conference. The local church may express certain desires that will be considered, but may not necessarily have its desires satisfied.

The third group is the *presbyterian* type, observed in the Presbyterian churches and in some Reformed churches. This form has a gradation of authority. The local church is run by the session, which is composed of the pastor and the elders. The presbytery is next in order of authority and includes a specified geographical area. This is superseded by the synod, which includes a larger geographical area, and finally the general assembly that has the ultimate authority for the church. In selecting a pastor, the local church will choose the man it desires, but its choice must be approved by the presbytery, the next larger authority.

In all three of these types, the property of the local church belongs to the larger group. In other words, the local church is not "autonomous," having self-government. In the presbyterian form a considerable amount of authority does reside within the local church, but it is still subject to the presbytery, synod and general assembly.

Fourth is the *congregational* form of government. This is found among Baptists, Disciples and The United Church of Christ, and to some extent among Lutherans. The Lutheran churches in some countries in Europe are under the jurisdiction of the government. In our country the synod has a good bit of authority over the local church, yet the local church makes its own decisions, calls its own pastor and on the whole guides its own activities.

As we study the New Testament, we believe we find in it a democratic form of government for the local church. There is evidence that the local group acted as a democracy on a number of different matters involving church life. I will mention five areas in which this democracy was expressed.

The first is found in 1 Corinthians 1:10, where the church is given the duty to preserve the unity of its fellowship. In Jude 3 the church has the responsibility to maintain pure doctrine and practice. In 1 Corinthians 11:23-24 it is to care for the conduct of the ordinances. In particular here it is the Lord's Supper. In Acts 1:23-26 and 6:3-5 it leads in the function of electing officers. It is interesting to notice that in Acts 14:23, where elders are ordained, the word translated "ordained" or "appointed" means "to designate by stretching out" or "pointing with the hand in voting," indicating that the pastors or the elders of the church were elected by the vote of the people. A fifth obligation is the necessity to exercise discipline. Jesus spoke of this obligation in Matthew 18:17, and Paul demanded it of the Corinthian church in 1 Corinthians 5. This is democracy in operation.

The local organization

We now must consider how the church will be organized to function efficiently and effectively. The task or mission of the church must always be kept uppermost in the minds of the leaders. It is easy to become sidetracked from the primary purpose into subsidiary activities. The church must ask, "Why are we here?" Then, "How can we best accomplish that task?" Here is where the function of the church becomes crucial.

The traditional approach in Baptist churches is to have pastoral leadership in conjunction with a deacon board that is the ruling body. There usually is a trustee board along with other official groups, such as Christian education, missions, social service, etc. These persons are elected annually by the church at large and serve for various terms such as three years. Often church officers are allowed to serve for a specified period of time, such as two three-year terms, and then must take at least a year's sabbatical from that office. Many Baptist churches function according to this pattern.

Some Baptist churches now utilize an elder board plan for church organization. That was the way Baptist churches were organized in their earliest history. This form of leadership has arisen anew in response to a desire for efficiency and the need to emphasize spiritual leadership, and as a result of study of the New Testament position of elder. Churches that have adopted this plan agree that the offices of pastor, elder and overseer are used interchangeably in the New Testament, but they see the plurality of elders as an important aspect of church function.

There are distinctions among elders largely based on 1 Timothy 5:17: "The elders who direct the affairs of the church well are worthy of double honor, especially those whose work is preaching and teaching." Distinctions are sometimes made between the preaching elders (pastors) and the ruling elders. It is clear from the earliest time in the book of Acts that those who were gifted to teach and preach were set aside for that task. As the church has developed, the expectations for modern pastors have become exceedingly high. Most churches want pastors to be scholars, administrators, effective communicators, visitors, coordinators, counselors and many other things. Pastors must be personable, must possess a love of people, be active in all sorts of community functions, faithful in their denominational fellowship and have a concern for every organization within the church. No pastor can ever perform all this. They and their churches must guard their loyalty to the main tasks. Occupation with the mundane can kill a pastor's effectiveness.

Because of these expectations the proper organization of the church is crucial. Each church must carefully, prayerfully and wisely make its own decisions about the proper organization for its own effectiveness. The local church is autonomous. It is not bound by any external organization, though it will wisely seek the counsel of others in its deliberations. Because it is a Baptist church, it will guide its deliberations according to accepted principles that are vital to the church.

It will first and foremost seek to be submissive to the headship of Jesus Christ. He is Lord of the church and Head of the body. He must be preeminent in all decisions the church makes. That will mean a prayerful church that is open to the prompting of the Spirit in its activity.

The church will seek to understand the teachings of the New Testament in policy decisions so that the many demands on the church in our contemporary society will be guided by biblical principles. The church must function in a rapidly changing world that desperately needs the good news of the gospel, but it must be true to the Bible.

The organization must take into account the universal priesthood of all believers that gives each believer equal access to God and thus to one another. Such a priesthood is always in community. In other words it is expressed, not individually, but in the church body. This is not to say that every decision made for the church must be made by the body as a whole. As the church grows, efficiency dictates that many decisions must be made by a board or council that has been given that responsibility. In most cases board or council members are elected or ratified by the church. The bottom line is that the church is the final authority.

It is here that some clarification is necessary. There are differences in the manner in which various churches elect or appoint their leaders and board members, and there are also differences in tenure. In some cases the elders and/or deacons are elected by the congregation. In other cases they are appointed by the governing board after a process of selection is fulfilled. In most cases the appointed leaders are ratified by the church as a whole. Tenure is another matter. In some cases the officer serves for a specified term, such as three years, and then must be reelected or reaffirmed. Certain churches specify a limited number of terms that may be served. Some churches appoint leaders for life, unless some unusual circumstance dictates ending the term. This is especially true for the elder. Their purpose is to give continuity. One church, in its desire for continuity but to avoid stagnation, affirms its elders for a two-year term and allows each to serve five two-year terms or ten years. Then they must take a year's sabbatical.

It is further important that the church and its leadership keep its mission uppermost in mind. However the church is organized it must reflect the fulfillment of its primary task. It is easy for those responsible for the spiritual oversight of the church to slip into a primary concern for the material and tangible. Buildings, budgets and resources are vitally important, but they can cloud the primary task of ministering to people and their needs.

All of this points up the need for quality of leadership. The biblical qualities for elders and deacons must be repeatedly brought to the attention of the church. Related to this is the giftedness of persons for the different roles necessary in the church. Sometimes a believer recognizes his or her own gifts and comes forward with desire and willingness to serve. At other times others in the church observe the giftedness of certain people and suggest they be elected or appointed to appropriate tasks.

One area that must be watched in church leadership is authority or authoritarianism. Authority is an earned quality. Just because a person is an elder does not necessarily carry with it accepted authority. Unfortunately sometimes churches have been harmed by those who hold office and act authoritatively without the accompanying authority given by the church. This usually happens because of a faulty usage of Hebrews 13:17: "Obey your leaders and submit to their authority. They keep watch over you as men who must give an account. Obey them so that their work will be a joy, not a burden, for that would be of no advantage to you." It is a mistake for leaders to take this text and demand obedience of the church. Those words are not written to the leaders, but to the people. Elders must consider Peter's words in 1 Peter 5:1-4, especially verse 3: "not lording it over those entrusted to you, but being examples to the flock." The leaders, the elders, must capture the genuine spirit of servanthood exhibited in the words of Peter but also from the Lord Jesus when He said: "You know that those who are regarded as rulers of the Gentiles lord it over them, and their high officials exercise authority over them. Not so with you. Instead, whoever wants to become great among you must be your servant, and whoever wants to be first must be slave of all. For even the Son of Man did not come to be served, but to serve, and to give his life as a ransom for many" (Mark 10:42-45). Genuine authority in the church takes place only through honest servanthood.

The successful church will be one that follows the principles enunciated in the New Testament and assumes its responsibility as a community of believers under the lordship of Christ. It does not function well over the long run if it is dominated by the whim of an individual or group.

Subsidiary organizations

We must not leave this chapter without some consideration of other organizations within the framework of the church. Are they legitimate in the light of New Testament principles?

We can safely say that other organizations within the framework of the church are legitimate—if they promote the total work of the church as outlined in the New Testament. What is that work? It is to preach and teach the gospel in order that the unreached might be reached with the good news of salvation. It is to train those who have become Christians in their faith and in their opportunities of service. It is to provide believers occasions for fellowship. This is all necessary in order that believers might be strengthened in conviction, that they might develop in their abilities to serve and that they might have friendships within the framework of the church. The Lord gave us capacities for social activity, such as healing the sick, feeding the hungry, caring for widows, the aged, orphans, and the poor. These must find their outlet within the wholesome environment of Christian fellowship.

Any organizations within the church that fulfill these purposes and do not violate any principles of the Word of God are legitimate. Examine the organizations of your church. Are they places to which you may bring outsiders who may not know Jesus Christ as Savior? Could outsiders find Him in this kind of fellowship? Or, at least, could these organizations be a means of leading in the direction of a decision? Do these organizations provide training in Christian living and knowledge of our faith? Are they places of wholesome fellowship to satisfy the normal gregarious instincts God has given? If they fulfill such purposes, these organizations are legitimate and can be used to the glory of the Lord.

9

The World Awaits Our Message

Expansion is endemic to the life of the church. It cannot remain isolated or ingrown. To be a cozy club of self-sufficient, self-satisfied people will only lead to deterioration for the church. That is contrary to its very nature. The church was intended to be an expanding and reaching community. There are several reasons for this.

The church was founded with a task to perform. This was evident from the very beginning when our Lord said, "I will build my church." He followed that by saying, "I will give you the keys of the kingdom of heaven; whatever you bind on earth will be bound in heaven, and whatever you loose on earth will be loosed in heaven" (Matthew 16:19). This is the church's task. It was crystallized in our Lord's concluding words on earth in the great commission (Matthew 28:18-20; Mark 16:15-16; Luke 24:45-49; Acts 1:8). That commission is for us as members of His church. In conjunction with these verses read Matthew 5:13-14. We are to be the salt of the earth and the light of the world. The importance of that task is almost too great to comprehend.

This mission arises out of *the nature of our Christian*

experience. When a person becomes a Christian, something radical takes place. The focal center of the believer's life is changed. The person of the world is self-centered. The Christian is Christ-centered. The Christ-centered person also becomes others-centered. He becomes concerned for the needs of others, and this means fulfilling the Lord's commission to the church.

This mission also arises out of *the nature of the church.* Our Lord founded His church to meet the needs of human life. People need fellowship, instruction in the truth, stability from a sense of belonging, and an outlet for service. This last is our primary concern in this chapter. No life has real value until the possessor of that life senses the opportunity to serve. The church provides this opportunity. The good news must be proclaimed around the world. That task cannot be performed by isolated Christians. The church fellowship is necessary to fulfill the mission our Lord gave.

Finally, *the nature of life* demands this mission. Normal life has a way of being expansive. It must share with others. When the life of the apostle Paul was transformed, he could not contain himself. He said, "I am obligated both to Greeks and non-Greeks, both to the wise and the foolish. That is why I am so eager to preach the gospel also to you who are at Rome" (Romans 1:14-15). Healthy life develops a burden for others. Where there is no burden, there is no value to living. To live is to serve. To live is to be dynamic. To live is to move. Unless we move we die, and to stop serving is to die. The church must serve to live. The New Testament church was a moving church. Nothing but death could stop the early Christians from advancing in their witness for Christ. The church that is a growing and moving church is a witnessing church.

It is greatly encouraging to observe the progress of the spread of the gospel in the world throughout the ages and especially in our century. The church gained ground slowly until the Middle Ages. In A.D. 1430 1 percent of the people in the world were Bible-believing Christians. By 1940 it was 3 percent, by 1983 7 percent and in 1993 10 percent. Today one in ten people are Bible-believing Christians. The most rapid growth for Protestantism has been in Latin America, Africa and Asia. Evangelicals have grown more rapidly than any other religious group.

These encouraging facts do not minimize the great need there is in our world for the good news about Jesus. The population of the world is about 5.5 billion and will be 6.5 billion by the year 2000. Of that population 1.734 billion claim to be Christian, of which 543 million are Protestant. There are 1.035 billion Muslim adherents in the world, largely located in the great belt of territory stretching from West Africa to Central and Southeast Asia. Islam is the fastest growing religion in the world today. That growth is largely because of their high birth rate. There is minimal growth through conversion.

We must further face the need of the Western world, once considered the cradle of Christianity. Europe and North America were the strongholds for the vitality of the church in the past. This is not true today. We have great need on these continents for a new thrust of church outreach in evangelism. In most of the European countries the vast majority of people are members of the church because of the state church system. But in many of these countries a bare 5 percent are actively involved in the church. In the United States nearly all mainline denominations have lost members in recent decades. For a period of years recently I was ministering in Southern California. When I researched the need in San Diego County, I found that 70 percent of the people were unchurched. This figure could be duplicated in many other sections of our country.

The church has a significant task before it. Evangelicals

all over the world are banding together to seek ways to reach the unreached peoples of the world by A.D. 2000. These are groups who have no knowledge of the gospel of Christ. These groups may be in remote areas of the world, but they may also be right in our cities in North America. It is estimated that there are 11,000 unreached people groups who need to hear the good news. Various denominations and churches are targeting particular groups as their unique responsibility. All of us in our individual churches must enter into this task.

How is this to be done? There is no easy answer because our world is changing so rapidly and so radically. Some of us have lived through a period of vast change. I am not quite pre-automobile, but almost. I remember in my childhood the first car my father purchased was a 1924 touring Nash. A regular sight at my home was the milkman coming down our alley with a horse-drawn wagon delivering milk. The first radio in our home was listened to through earphones. I recall seeing television demonstrated at the Minnesota State Fair but could not fathom the possibility of its presence as a common appliance in every home. I could mention much more, but this emphasizes the rapid changes that we are all experiencing.

If this seems startling, listen to the futurists. They are saying that the knowledge we possess now, as great as it is, is only 3 percent of what will be available in 2010. That is not many years away. That blows our minds.

How does the church respond to this startling situation when it is commissioned to bring the gospel to the whole world? Our tendency is to respond rather simplistically and say, "The gospel message of 2000 years ago has not changed, and we must share that with the world." This is essentially true. The great fact that God has invaded human history in the coming of Jesus Christ is fantastic good news. He came in order to penetrate the life of each individual so that each one can know the transforming power of His presence. We concur that the gospel is steady and unchangeable in this changing world. On the other hand, the packaging of that gospel needs to change in order to touch the people of our contemporary society. That is true not only in our own communities but also all over the world. How we package the unchangeable gospel will vary with our location and the culture where we find ourselves.

Let us try to think about the world and its characteristics in order to better understand the packaging process. Consider an analogy. In the industrial world we find a differentiation between the manufacturing mentality and the marketing mentality. The manufacturing mentality says, "Produce a better product and you will always sell it." The marketing mentality says, "Check out the market to see what is needed, then produce that product and you will always sell it." The manufacturing mentality says, "Produce a better mousetrap and you will always have a sale for it." The marketing mentality says, "Go and find out who needs mousetraps before you produce them. Then you will sell them."

In a very real sense the church needs both mentalities. It has the perfect product—the good news. It also must possess the marketing concern to discover how best to package that good news. The whole world needs that good news. But many times they cannot see the importance of our message because we have not packaged it well.

Some of the strongest and fastest growing churches in our country and around the world have captured this understanding. They have utilized marketing techniques and researched the yearnings and needs of people to present the gospel in terms both understood and meaningful. Examine churches like Wooddale in Eden Prairie, Minnesota, New Hope in Portland, Oregon, and Willow Creek in South Barrington, Illinois. One can also see this in other countries as well, as in Seoul, Korea, and Sao Paulo, Brazil.

Each local church must find its own best way to share the message of Christ in its own community and around the world. No group can do it for another. But all of us can look at some of the general characteristics of the world and see how the gospel responds to these characteristics and needs.

An anonymous society

The world in which we live is strange. Population is burgeoning, but the more it grows the more people feel isolated and alone. Check it out in our large cities. The more people there are the more isolated people feel. There is even a planned isolation. People avoid involvement. Many of you know what I am saying because you have little contact with your own neighbors. Most people seem to like it this way.

Two men worked in the same factory, although in different departments. They passed each other occasionally but never spoke. One day one of them asked for a certain day off because his daughter was getting married. A little later the other man asked for the same day off because his son was getting married. When the two arrived at the church for the wedding, they discovered they had worked in the same factory for years but had never met or spoken to one another. That may be a little extreme, but it speaks to the anonymity of our world.

Loneliness will become even more widespread as time goes on. The traditional family is dead. Marriage is an outdated institution in the minds of many. We have become a nation of friendless adults. We studiously avoid connecting with other people.

As prevalent as anonymity and loneliness are, people

still yearn for love and friendship. In the United States, as well as in other nations, the longing for strong friendships far exceeds the answer. This yearning is observed in contemporary music. Listen to the lyrics of most popular songs. They are loaded with sighs for genuine love and friendship. Discover the longing in contemporary literature, and in dramas seen on the screen, TV or the stage. Genuine lonesomeness is a tragedy found all over the world.

God created human beings with social inclinations. We want to be with one another. The way we act in this world is a paradox. We want to be anonymous, yet we yearn for friendship and real love. Recent surveys suggest four primary goals people have. All of them relate to being happy. The very first one is that we want to be loved.

It is to this goal that the church can respond most helpfully. No other group of people or institution in our society can respond more meaningfully to this need to be loved and to love. The deepest form of loving and caring comes from God. That is why the most familiar verse of the Bible is John 3:16. But the love of God is not an abstract idea only to be written or talked about. It is not merely a theory or some lofty philosophical idea. The love of God is discovered in relationships. It is experienced through friendly loving relationships with others who have already experienced the love of God.

Loving outreach by the church takes effort. We do not easily move out to the unknown. This loving friendship must be expressed in two directions. It should be shown within the church as well as beyond the church. We are all needy human beings yearning to be loved and to love, both inside and outside the church. It is amazing how easy it is to miss this within the church.

I was once invited to speak at an unfamiliar church. My wife and I left early enough to be sure to find it. When we arrived no one was at the church. We took a walk. When we came back the pastor was there and I joined him in his study. My wife went to the sanctuary. It was early, and just two women sat in the pews. She asked if it was OK for her to sit with them. They said certainly and moved over, but neither said another word to her. When the service began the pastor and I came to the platform and he introduced my wife to the congregation. At the close of the service the two women nearly tripped over one another to greet my wife. But when she first came in she was a stranger, and they let her remain a stranger. That is not an uncommon experience in churches. We really haven't realized how important it is for us to learn the fact of the lonesomeness of our society and the need for friendship and love.

This loving concern must extend itself beyond the church. A church in California had about 100 members when a loving pastor came on the scene. He taught the people by example and by teaching what it was to extend friendship to the outsider. In 20 years that church had grown to more than 2000 members. Nearby was a like evangelical church that also had had a membership of 100. After 20 years it still had 100 members. The one church learned what outreach through friendship could do while the other did not.

The book by Kathi Mills, *Broken Members, Mended Body*, tells the story of New Hope Community Church in Portland, Oregon, pastored by Dale Galloway. On Christmas Sunday 1970, Dale Galloway preached as a broken man in his church in Oregon. The previous Friday a stranger had come to the door and served him with divorce papers from his wife. Within 24 hours he was at the airport bidding good-bye to his wife of 13 years and his two children, eight and five years old, all of whom he loved dearly. In a sense, it was the perfect family. Then suddenly he had lost it all.

After ranting and raving and turning his anger on God,

Galloway finally came to the point of realizing that he could not go on without God's help. He asked God to forgive him for his failures and for his rebellion against Him. Then he placed his life once more in God's hands. At that moment he seemed to hear the Lord say to him, "Surely I will be with you always, to the very end of the age."

He was 31 years of age. He had pastored two churches successfully and now was in a large church of his denomination in Oregon. Upon learning of the divorce, a denominational leader told Galloway he could not continue in pastoral ministry. That was another shattering experience, for he possessed a deep sense of call to ministry. In October of 1972 he began a church with no resources, no funds, no people. He had nothing but the dream that he should be ministering. He started in a drive-in theater. Today New Hope Community Church of Portland has more than 5000 members. It is built on the whole approach of ministering hope and love to hurting people in the name of Jesus Christ.

Kathi Mills was there observing the many facets of the church to write the book. On Monday night she attended a New Life Victorious meeting. She arrived a little early and found the room set up with more than 300 chairs. She could not imagine 300 people coming to a church meeting on a Monday night. Most churches have difficulty getting 300 people present on Sunday morning, she thought. Quickly the place filled. They had to set up more chairs in the overflow area. This was a meeting where people from small groups shared their hurts, troubles and brokenness. It was the kind of event that helped one realize that true joy in Jesus Christ is indestructible. Even the most difficult hurts in life cannot overcome the inner joy that is present in one who has met Jesus Christ.

In our anonymous society the church that discovers the hunger of people for love and friendship and extends itself in answering that yearning will have great success in seeing people transformed. The love of Jesus Christ will become real.

A mobile society

It only takes a quick observation to know that we live in a very mobile society worldwide. In the United States one in five families moves every year. In some communities it is one in two. Not only do people change residences frequently, but a majority of us are on the move regularly by the demands of work, family or recreation. In all parts of the world a number of factors create the mobility we are observing. Famine, earthquakes, floods or war fracture societies and cause people to migrate from one place to another. All of this mobility creates a terrible sense of insecurity and instability.

A settled community gave an undergirding of stability and security. Neighbors knew one another and supported one another whenever trouble arose. Some of us were reared in that kind of geographical community and delighted in its support. Mobility has ripped that from us. It is gone. With it went the normal human support system we once knew. Stability and security faded with the loss of geographical community.

Human beings find their community in various ways. Instead of geographical community, many today find community in common interest or common function groupings. These relate to the things people do and are interested in. It may be a recreational interest or a vocational function. Interest or vocational groupings may be good, but they may be quite temporary and volatile. The sense of security in such a community cannot be strong. People may still be floundering, yearning for a solid and strong support system for life. The reality is that the mobility of society is not going to stop.

It is here that the community of the church becomes the answer. Our Lord founded the church to respond to the needs of people. He knows that men and women need a support system in a community. The one place where genuine community can be found is in the church. An answer to the need for security and stability is part of the gospel. It is good news for unstable people that they may find support within the church. In Hebrews 10:25 the apostle was led to recognize this and say, "Let us not give up meeting together, as some are in the habit of doing, but let us encourage one another—and all the more as you see the Day approaching."

The importance of community was seen in New Testament days. Even in the small community of the apostles it was observed. Only one fell away. That was Judas Iscariot. It is rare that someone loses out in life when he is part of a community. It is when a person withdraws himself from the community that he finds trouble.

During World War II I was in the Navy. One day standing in line for a meal a fellow sailor who had been in the Navy for a while sidled up to me and began to talk. He asked if I was a Christian. I said yes. He replied that he thought so because he had seen me pray before meals. I got acquainted with him and discovered he had no sense of Christian friendship or community in the Navy up to that point. He had become a Christian earlier in life but was about ready to give it up and was floundering. We began attending church together and he discovered the strength of the community of the church. Through the church he met a lovely young Christian woman. They later married. Some years ago I was preaching in a church in another part of the country. At one of the sessions, a dinner meeting, a trio sang. It was this man's wife and two daughters. Stability had come to him through the community of the church.

Many of us are awed at the growth of the Crystal Cathedral in Garden Grove, Calif. Some years ago I was invited to their week-long leadership conference. What surprised me was the impact of this church's small groups. Every meal featured a testimony by someone in the church. No one spoke of the significance of the preaching of Robert Schuler. They all told how their group had ministered to them in their hurts and led them to faith in Christ.

As a church we must recognize the mobile society in which we live that creates instability and insecurity. The church is the one community in the world that has the potential of meeting this need worldwide. We must tap into ways of bringing struggling persons into the community of stability by touching them at their points of interest and/or function. What a task!

A nonrational society

Nonrational may seem like a strange way to describe our world today. But examine how we are functioning. Look at the telltale signs that indicate who we are. We seem to be enamored of the nonrational. One can see it in art, whether it be on the canvas or in three-dimensional expressions. Abstract art has an appeal to it because you can put your own interpretation on it. In fact the artist doesn't intend to give an interpretation to the work. The artist is just giving expression to what we are as a society.

One can see it in poetry. Some of us were reared largely on poetry that had rhythm and rhyme. There was a rationale to it. I do not mean that I don't appreciate contemporary poetry with its different expressions, but it has nuances that are not as rational to grasp as before.

The nonrational also may be observed in advertising. Watching TV commercials, one is often startled by the disconnectedness between what is shown and the product being promoted. We really learn nothing about the product, but are drawn to it by the attention-getter. It is quite nonrational.

Unfortunately the non-rational may be noticed in religion as well. We are easily attracted to religious response by what is largely a feeling level of life. In many cases we have adopted the dictum, "If it feels good, it must be right." The normative in religion for many becomes very subjective.

But the nonrational in life creates a strange vacuum in the minds of people. An emptiness happens. An unsatisfied yearning occurs.

Some years ago I was on a sabbatical leave at Yale University Divinity School in New Haven, Conn. During the lenten season I was asked to lead a Bible study for a couple of weeks in the absence of the regular teacher. This was in one of the Protestant churches in the center on the green. I asked the question, "Who is God?" The woman who taught the junior high students in that church answered, "I believe God is expressed in human relationships. Wherever people are related to one another there God is. If all human beings were gone from this earth except one, God would be gone." That was an altogether new definition of God for me. Another woman replied, "God is wherever I find truth." Notice how she said that. It is wherever *she* found truth. That meant she became the judge of truth and thus of who God is. A third woman said, "God is the creation of man in the Judeo-Christian religion. Just like all other religions in the world, it is man's creation that gives us God." There were men present in this class, but as it happened the women were the ones responding at this particular point. A fourth woman said, "I create my own God." Then she paused a moment and admitted, "Well, maybe something created me, but really I create my own God."

Now note, I did not ask this question about who God is down on the street corner. This occurred in a voluntary Bible study in the middle of the week in a Protestant church. There was a real vacuum of meaning in these statements. On the other hand they expressed a great yearning to know and understand. These people chose to come to the Bible study. They were seeking something to satisfy their minds.

In spite of the nonrational world in which we live, there is a longing to understand. God has given us intellectual capacities and we yearn to have meaning for life. Isaiah said, "'Come now, let us reason together,' says the Lord. 'Though your sins are like scarlet, they shall be as white as snow; though they are red as crimson, they shall be as wool.'"

The baby boomers are searching intensely for purpose in life. It is quite possible that the following generation will increase its desire for meaning and understanding as well.

Here the church has significant responsibility and opportunity. We must seize the day. In a special survey recently taken, 62 percent of the respondents said the church is not relevant. But just because they think this, we must not assume that they are not looking for a word from God from the Bible. That is exactly what they are looking for. We must ever be aware that the Bible is relevant. We just need to know its relevance, understand it and then package it in contemporary language so that people receive with clarity the word from God.

To live perpetually in the nonrational does not satisfy. The hunger for meaning and understanding in life is strong. The church has great opportunity to respond to that hunger with effective Bible studies, relevant educational programs and clear preaching of the great life-changing themes of the Bible.

Outreach must be a big part of the life of the church. It must feel a global concern for the unbelieving world. The church must be responsive to the local situation in which it finds itself. Local churches can learn from what other effective churches are doing but can never replicate another church. Each one must find its own mission and fulfill it.

10

How and Why
to Participate

A layman was introduced to a pastor in a casual meeting on the street. "Where is your church?" he asked. "When do you mean?" responded the pastor. The layman replied with some surprise, "Well, right now." The pastor then answered, "It is in the bakery, in the school, in the business office and in the shop." "No," said the layman, "I meant your building." "That is at 2nd Street and 2nd Avenue," the pastor observed, "but that is not really my church." The church is people. We know that. It is not the building. The church is wherever the believer happens to be. The church can be scattered as well as gathered. We are much more conscious of the church when it is gathered than when it is scattered.

Because of this basic truth the involvement of the church takes on very special significance: the involvement of each individual within the church. No believer can isolate himself from the church. It is a temptation when talking about the church to refer to the church as "it" or "they." We are the church. We are the church whether we are gathered or scattered. This implies a special responsibility for each of us, since we are the church.

The Bible clearly enunciates the responsible trust that has been committed to us by God. That trust involves our total person, our abilities, our handling of time and our resources. The Bible is a book of trust given. Our first parents were given the responsibility of the Garden of Eden. Because they were poor managers, they were put out of the garden. The accounts of Abraham and Lot, his nephew, are stories of responsibility given. Abraham succeeded gloriously while Lot was an abysmal failure. The book of Jonah tells the story of the sacred trust God gave the prophet to bring a message to a great city. At first Jonah was untrue to that trust. When he repented and proceeded to discharge the terms of his responsibility, success came to him in a manner and measure that dumbfounded him.

The New Testament abounds with instances where individuals were expected to assume responsibility for a trust they had been given. In our English Bibles, this trust is expressed by a number of different words, all coming from the same Greek term. Let us look at a few of the places where the expression is found: 1) Matthew 20:8—the parable about the *foreman* of a vineyard; 2) Luke 12:42—another parable concerning one who was made *manager* of a wealthy person's household; 3) Luke 16:1ff.—another becomes *manager* of a business; 4) 1 Corinthians 9:17; Ephesians 3:2; Colossians 1:25—a particular *task* or a *mission* to perform; 5) Romans 16:23—one is a *director* or *treasurer* of a city; 6) Galatians 4:2—a *guardian* or *trustee* of a child. All of these terms were translated steward or stewardship in earlier versions of the Bible. The idea is that one has been given responsibility, and an accountability is demanded. This involves the whole personality, including one's talents, time and treasure.

Our talents

The Bible is the revelation of the Lord of life and His relation to us in our human experience. All that we are and all that we have belong to the Lord. Someone may quickly ask, "Why should I give my talents to Christ? I have worked hard for them. I have sought to develop myself. Why should He have them?"

There are several reasons our talents belong to the Lord. First, *the Christian must remember his new relationship.* The believer is a changed person, with a new Master. In 1 Corinthians 6:19 we read, "You are not your own." We no longer belong to ourselves. We belong to the Lord. There is a sense in which we never did belong to ourselves. The unbeliever is self-centered, but his self-centeredness demands that he give himself to something as the master of his life. Believers have changed the lord of their lives. We have a new Lord. He has purchased us, and we develop a love to do His will.

Possibly a story from Charles Dickens' *A Tale of Two Cities* will help us grasp the significance of what our Lord has done for us. Charles Darnay was in the dungeon prison awaiting death by the guillotine during the French Revolution. Sidney Carton, his English friend and a lawyer who had dissipated his life, gained access to the prison to visit his friend the night before his death. He told Charles to exchange clothes with him. He was going to take Charles' place at the guillotine, he told him. He had little reason to live because of the way he had wasted his life; Charles, on the other hand, had a family that needed him. Finally Charles Darnay acceded to his persuasion and exchanged clothing with Sidney. Charles Darnay walked out of the prison under the name of Sidney Carton. The next day Sidney Carton went to the guillotine and died under the name of Charles Darnay.

When Jesus went to the cross and died, He did so under

your name and mine. It was not for any sin of His that He died but for your sin and mine. He did it to set us free, but bonded us to Him in a love that transforms our whole life. When we accept Him, we have a brand new relationship.

This new relationship gives us a new obligation (Romans 12:1-2). It is our "reasonable service" (KJV) to commit ourselves to the Lord. This phrase could well be translated "intelligent worship," for it is an intelligent relationship. It is the logic of Christianity. We do not serve to win His favor. We do so because we have received His favor, and we serve in gratitude and love. This is in complete contrast to service before becoming a Christian. Service before was the pressure of an external law of duty or to achieve favor. Service now results from an internal love because of Christ's mercy to us.

Think of it this way. One evening you are walking quietly home from your place of business. Suddenly the fire siren startles you. Your heart leaps with fear as the thought of home and loved ones flashes upon you. As you near your home your worst fears are realized. Your house is in flames! You rush over and find your wife and children have been saved except one little one who is yet in the building. The next instant a brave fireman hurries past and, dashing into the burning house, finds his way to the little one. He carries her out through the flames and smoke and puts her in your arms. The baby is safe, but the fireman has been critically burned.

A period of time goes by, and this fireman finds himself in need. He then comes to your home, and standing before you he shows his hands and body and says, "Look at this expression of my sacrifice for you in these scarred hands and face and scorched feet. I have a need now. I appeal to you to help me." There is nothing in the world that you would not give to that man. What about Jesus Christ? He shows us what He has done for us. Ought we not give ourselves to Him?

This leads us to another attitude in this new relationship. It is a love relationship. Considering the preceding passages and also John 15:13-16, we recognize this relationship of love. To love the Lord with our complete personality is more important than anything we might give to Him of our possessions (Mark 12:33). Our emotions are God-given. The capacity for love is of God, but it ought to be expressed to Him. Our emotions link us with the object of our love. If we love the world, some sin, or friends, whether good or bad, we become linked to them. If we love the Lord we become linked to Him and give Him all of our talent because of our new relationship.

Second, we give Him all of our talent because *He is the source of our abilities* (1 Corinthians 4:7). Every ability we have is from the Lord. Even health to use our capacities is a gift from God. Stop and think a moment. Who gave the money that was necessary to develop your skills? Who gave the energies to develop your capacities? Who gave the opportunities to enter school for training? All is from God. Abilities that God has given are a trust. Every one of us has some talent. These faculties have been given by God to be used to His glory.

A third reason for letting the Lord use all of our talents is *the need of the world and the need of the church.* We have previously studied the need of the world. The need can be met only as the church proclaims Jesus Christ. But the need of the church is only met as individuals become part of its service and function. In Romans 1:14 the apostle Paul considered himself under obligation to all people. He was under obligation because of all he had received, but also because of the needs of a common humanity.

We also are under obligation. To whom are you obliged? Where are you using your energies? You are using them somewhere. Many give themselves completely to their business or study or profession because they are convinced that their best ought to be given to the tasks before them. Have you ever considered that your best should be given to Christ? Some give much of themselves to secular organizations other than their business. Is that right when the needs of the world and church are so great? Your local church needs everything you can give to it—in balance with family and employment.

Long ago a missionary from India told of seeing an Indian mother going to the Ganges River. In her arms she clasped a sickly, deformed child. Clinging to her garment was a healthy, perfectly formed child. Later the missionary saw the mother with just the sickly one. The other child was gone, and the missionary realized what had taken place. Curiously he asked "Why didn't you throw the deformed child to the crocodiles?" Haughtily the woman answered, "We give our best to the gods." What a tragic expression of futile devotion. But what an illustration of complete surrender.

Think of your own abilities. Then consider the needs of the church. We must give ourselves to the Lord's work. Some ask, "But what can I do?" The opportunities of service within the church are so varied it is difficult to list them all. One can sing, play an instrument, teach, give Christian literature to seekers, invite people to services, work with boys and girls clubs, help with the social events of an organization, be a friend to someone, visit a shut-in, do office work, usher, use a trade, do accounting, manage the facilities, bring flowers to the church, send a card to someone in need, or use one of many more opportunities to serve through one's church.

Are you hiding your abilities from usefulness in the work of the Lord? When Luigi Tarisio was found dead there was hardly a comfort found in his home, but hidden in his attic were 246 exquisite violins. While Luigi had treasured his collection, he had robbed the world of some of its sweetest music. Some of the violins had been hoarded by others before him. When the greatest Stradivarius was first played, it had been silent for 147 years!

As a Christian you have some ability. Are you allowing that talent to lie dormant and, thus, preventing a songless world from experiencing the spiritual harmony and melody that Christ can bring? Your service and the use of your talents may do that for someone. Ask, as the apostle Paul did, "What shall I do, Lord?" (Acts 22:10).

Our time

You may not be wealthy in material possessions, but in time you are as rich as anyone else. The president of our country with all of his responsibilities has no more time than the rest of us. The president of the greatest corporation has no more time than I have. Inequalities arise in the way time is used.

Because we are Christians, we must consider how we make use of our time. We see this first because of *the emphasis in the Bible.* Throughout the Bible we find repeated demands upon people to observe the value of time. Never is the use of time treated lightly in the Bible. Here are some passages worthy of your study: Psalm 89:47; Proverbs 27:1; Ecclesiastes 3:1,17; Isaiah 55:6; Luke 19:43-44; John 9:4 and 12:35; 1 Corinthians 7:29; 2 Corinthians 6:2; Ephesians 5:14-16; Colossians 4:5. All of these passages place real claim upon us concerning our use of time.

We must also be careful in our use of time because it cannot be recovered. Once it is gone it is gone! It constantly moves whether we do or not. Time is much like the movement of a river that we observe from a bridge. It keeps flowing toward the ocean. We look at a bit of water and can imagine it moving on to the next city and then to the next and on and on until it is swallowed up in the ocean. It never stops. That is the same with time. Once it is gone, it can never be retrieved.

Mythology pictures opportunity as a bald man with one tuft of hair at the front of his head. He is always moving forward. If you are to catch opportunity, you must catch him by the hair the moment he presents himself, because once he has gone by it is impossible to grasp him. The back of his head is bald.

There is something agonizing about this matter of time and opportunity. Yet it makes us aware that we must surrender our lives and our time more completely to Jesus Christ. How do you use your time? How much time do you spend looking at TV ? How much time just sitting and doing nothing? How much time sleeping? What about your reading? Do you waste time reading that which is of little value?

Maybe this sounds unreasonable. It may seem that I think no one can have any relaxation. That isn't the question. Everyone needs diversion and relaxation. The question is, what is relaxing? Just a waste of time is not relaxing —it's often wearing. When there is real relaxation, time is valuably used. As Christians each of us must guard how our time is used because it cannot be recovered.

Again we must seriously reflect on our use of time because of *the urgency of life.* Earthly life is a temporary arrangement. But the decisions of life are permanent. The temporary nature of this life emphasizes the value of time. Death comes quickly and perhaps suddenly. Sometimes the healthiest person may have a short life span. We must use every opportunity in constructive living and service for the glory of Christ.

A former Duke of Buckingham cried as he was concluding a life that had been devoted to folly and sin: "Oh, what a prodigal I have been of the most valuable of all possessions—time! I have squandered it away with the persuasion that it was lasting, and now, when a few days would be worth a hecatomb of worlds, I cannot flatter myself with the prospect of a half a dozen hours."

When Salmasius, one of the greatest of scholars of his time, drew near to death, he exclaimed bitterly against himself: "Oh, I have lost a world of time: time, the most precious thing on the earth, whereof if I had one more year, it should be spent in David's Psalms and Paul's epistles. Oh, mind the world less and God more!"

Life is urgent and time is valuable. We must remind ourselves of Paul's word in Ephesians 5:16: "...making the most of every opportunity, because the days are evil." We are managers of our time. We have as much time as anyone else—and we are accountable to God for the use of it.

Our treasure

We are also managers of our material possessions. Of the Macedonian Christians' liberality in sending a gift for the work of the Lord, Paul says, "They did not do as we expected, but they gave themselves first to the Lord and then to us in keeping with God's will" (2 Corinthians 8:5). As we give ourselves, we too will give of what we possess.

We are accountable for all that we have, for God has given it. We are accountable for the amount we give to the Lord's work, and we are accountable for the places to which we give. Many do not realize their responsibility in how and where they give their money. We are further responsible for the amount we keep and what we do with that. Our management does not concern merely the tithes and offerings for the Lord's work. Our responsibility concerns all that we possess. It must grieve the Lord to see the way some people spend their money after giving a tithe. A good barometer for our spiritual life is the way we handle our possessions.

In the first place we deny *God's sovereignty* if we do not practice a careful trust with our possessions. He is the Creator. All that we have and all that we are has originally come from God. Read Psalm 8 and be reminded of God's greatness and our littleness. It seems we are too much under the influence of pagan ideas. We constantly drive to gain more for ourselves. We have lost the biblical sense of responsibility to God. Remember the practice of the jubilee year in the Old Testament period. It came once every 50 years and at that time all property went back to its original owner. Whenever a person purchased property, he knew it would return to the original owner in the jubilee year. This was a graphic way of reminding the people that everything originally came from God. If we are unfaithful trustees of our possessions, we deny God's sovereignty—for He is Lord of all, including our possessions.

In the second place, a failure to practice good management is a denial of *God's Word.* The Bible teaches that at least one-tenth of our income is to be given to the Lord for His work. This was a universal law that preceded the giving of the law to Moses at Mount Sinai and has continued to the present time. Abraham observed it 700 years before Moses ever received the law. Jacob observed it 500 years before the law was given. Remember that Christ fulfilled the law. He did not do away with it. When we became Christians, we received a higher law that rules our lives (Romans 8:2). This higher law ought to express itself in a higher ideal than the law given in the Old Testament. No Christian who really understands his glorious experience can give less than 10 percent.

The apostle Paul says in 1 Corinthians 16:2 that we ought to give systematically. Anyone who gives systematically must consider the percentage to be given as well as the regularity of giving.

Third, if we are not faithful trustees of our treasure, we

deny *God's love.* Read John 3:16; 2 Corinthians 8:9; Philippians 2:5-8 to discover how much Christ has done for us out of His love for us.

He is the Creator, and yet He became a babe weak enough to be carried in the arms of a woman. He who is the King of all kings was born in a manger of poor parentage. He who is the Creator of all had no place He could call His home, for He said, "Foxes have holes and birds of the air have nests, but the Son of Man has no place to lay his head." He who had all of the angels bow in homage before Him was willing to take a towel and bow before the apostles and wash their feet. He who created the oceans of the world had to ask for a drink. He who created every harvest field of all ages had to ask for bread. He who had created all things permitted weak human beings to crucify Him. He who should have the richest diadem placed upon His brow as the King of kings allowed men to press the crown of thorns upon His brow. Think of all He has done for us.

Again, our neglect of giving to the Lord's work is a denial of *God's goodness.* Read carefully the following passages: Proverbs 3:9-10; 11:24-25; Malachi 3:10-11; Luke 6:38; 2 Corinthians 9:6-7. In each of these, God promises greater return than we have given. To refuse to give a tithe, at least, is to deny the Lord's goodness and make Him a liar. It is almost like the man who remembered at breakfast that it was his wife's birthday so he kissed her and went downtown and bought himself a new suit of clothes. God rains the wealth of heaven upon us. Then we go out and buy another automobile and enlarge our business, and God is forgotten. Many will testify that God's goodness is beyond compare when we obey Him in our giving.

In the last place, to fail to recognize our material responsibility is to deny *God's commission.* God gave all of us a mission to perform. We are Christians because someone fulfilled God's commission in bringing the gospel to us.

Who is going to receive the gospel because *we* have fulfilled that commission? Money is needed to do it. In our own country there has been an increase in giving to Christian work nearly every year in recent decades. This sometimes encourages us.

But there are some disturbing things as well. One is that there has been a drop in the percentage of the charitable dollar that goes to religious purposes. Another is that the increase in giving is not as great as the increase in income. A third is that the increase in giving is not as great as the decrease in purchasing power of the dollar. And a fourth disturbing thing is that the amount we are spending for things far less important is so out of proportion to our giving to the Lord's work. For example, consider the amount we spend on recreation and entertainment as well as luxury items compared to our giving to the Lord's work around the world.

Wherever we turn there is a crying need for the gospel, and to send it forth requires more money. As we conclude this chapter remember Paul's word in 1 Corinthians 4:2: "Now it is required that those who have been given a trust must prove faithful."

11

Fellowship and Working with Others

"Fellowship" is the word that best expresses the relationship of believers within a Baptist church and of churches with one another. Baptists do not constitute a denomination in a strict sense of that word. They are churches voluntarily cooperating in a common bond of faith and service. Our understanding of the New Testament churches is that they worked together to fulfill the mission of Christ. Human nature, as God created us, demands such relationships. Human beings long for fellowship and depend on others in every area of activity. In the spiritual realm there is no better way to meet this ever-present need of people for fellowship than by banding together as cooperating local churches.

The concerns of this chapter are varied. The individual needs relationships, and these are found within the local church. Local churches need fellowship, and that is found in the larger group that we have come to call a denomination. Even beyond that there is a larger fellowship of working together with groups of other denominations who are of like faith on the basic issues of the Bible.

On the local church level

Local churches arise because believers in Christ in one geographical area get together, recognizing their *need for Christian fellowship*. This social spirit of human beings is observed wherever people are found. Persons of like mind in other activities of life get together. When immigrants from another land come to this country, they tend to live with their own people. In like manner believers find one another and form local churches.

This may readily be observed in the biblical pattern in both Old and New Testaments. The word used for the assembly of the people in the Old Testament had a meaning similar to that of the word used in the New Testament. The word *ecclesia*, translated church in the New Testament, was used frequently in the Greek translation of the Old Testament.

Old Testament people had a central place for worship in the tabernacle and then in the three temples that followed. As the people dispersed, they recognized the need for something more than the central temple. Thus came the rise of the synagogue. In each locality where a group of Jewish people came together to worship they formed a synagogue. The existence of their nation depended upon their worship in the synagogue and in the temple. When they forsook their worship, they were led into captivity.

In the New Testament we see that Christ went regularly to the synagogue on the Sabbath Day "as was his custom." When He founded the church, He provided for the needed fellowship for believers. The writer to the Hebrews warned believers against neglecting united worship when he said in chapter 10, verse 25, "Let us not give up meeting together, as some are in the habit of doing." Throughout the book of Acts the believers assembled together for fellowship, the breaking of bread and worship. The Bible constantly impresses us with the need of the local church fellowship.

Again it is observed in the human *need for vital relationships*. Friendships are crucial to maintain our convictions. Our Lord, knowing our human characteristics, provided the church to meet this need. There is support in genuine friendship. When one moves from one locality to another, the best place to form new friendships is in the local church. It was such a move that led me, as a young man, to my conversion experience.

The welfare of the family depends on this fellowship. It promotes family life like nothing else in the world. The family is the backbone of the nation. Examine what will develop the family and you will always be driven back to the basic influence of the church. This is illustrated in the pioneering days of the West. Invariably towns that had churches thrived, while those without churches died away.

A third need met by the local church is the *need for stability of life*. A sense of security can come to those who belong to a local church. The feeling of belonging is necessary for human character. Because the church is stable, we find stability. The Christian finds the church a place of encouragement and comfort in times of need. One finds in it instruction for morality and for the development of a good life. Light is given on truths that ought to be known. Convictions are strengthened in those areas where the individual has already determined the truth.

A fourth is the *need to serve*. We have already considered the significance of service for an individual and the ways by which one might serve. And the very fact of membership is service. It puts one's approval on the work of the church. That becomes a witness in itself. A person's regular attendance encourages others to attend. Even in these ways one is serving, and the church provides the outlet. A believer must serve to really live. Fulfilling avenues of service are readily available in the church.

More than that, the church directs young lives into

places of full-time service for Christ. One of the thrilling experiences for a church is to see one of its young people answer the call of God to Christian service. A new zest comes to a church that commissions one of its young people for the mission field or says farewell to another who is entering a Christian school to begin training for service for Christ. We are keenly aware how much we need one another in the local church.

The denominational level

Even as individuals need fellowship with one another, churches need fellowship with other churches. Concrete illustrations of this can be found by talking to a pastor or a worker in an "independent" church—a church without any kind of association. The ordination of young men for Christian service is an example. On several occasions I have been among a number of pastors requested to come to a council to consider ordaining some young man in an independent church. The local church could ordain the man, but it did not feel a freedom to ordain without considering the counsel of others.

There are several purposes for the larger fellowship of churches. One purpose is to share the *common faith* (Ephesians 4:3-6; 1 Corinthians 12:12-13). A common faith in Jesus Christ draws churches of Baptist persuasion together. The churches belonging to this fellowship are united in a voluntary association, but that association is vital for spiritual health and vigorous function as churches. The oneness expressed in the Ephesian and Corinthian passages is felt by these churches. There is an "inevitableness" about being together. It is evident that churches cannot go it alone. Our faith is a social faith, and leadership is necessary. That has led to organizational development and the selection of leaders to ensure and encourage that common bond. Delegates of the churches cooperatively select officers for the various ministries of the denominational fellowship. Being one in Christ can be expressed through vital participation in a larger fellowship of churches.

Further, churches unite because of *common interests.* They need one another for counsel. That makes them more effective as witnesses. That makes the wisdom and experience of many available to all. This same situation can be seen in the New Testament. On certain issues it was necessary to gather leaders of various churches together to determine what would be the will of God. Read Acts 15 about the Jerusalem council. That council in a sense was the beginning of what we now would call a denominational fellowship. The representatives and leaders of the churches came together to discuss the issues at stake. Their decisions were communicated both by letter and by messengers to the churches. Those decisions became determinative for the life of the whole church and of the individual churches. Frequently pastors and churches need the counsel of others to function effectively. For that reason participation in a larger fellowship is a valuable and necessary aid to church life.

Then again a denominational fellowship is necessary because of a *common work.* Our mission as believers and as local churches is worldwide. We cannot do it effectively alone. District conferences aid local churches in their task in their geographical areas. One church cannot do all that needs to be done even in its local area. Take, for example, summer camp for boys, girls, teens and families. This work is an invaluable tool in reaching people for Jesus Christ and for service for Christ. Most churches could not operate a camp on their own, but several churches working together can maintain an effective program. All across the land are areas that need new churches with a gospel witness. By our united labors much more is achieved in starting new lighthouses for Christ than could be achieved by single churches.

This area-wide fellowship increases our sense of strength. United activities are an encouragement to local women's, men's and youth groups. Some local churches are small. The groups within them may be small and united activity strengthens participants' convictions and enthusiasm. Teens and young adults especially need the impact of these united activities. Christian youth too frequently feel they are an exceedingly small minority.

The work of Baptist fellowships extends across the United States and into many other countries. Each fellowship maintains world mission programs that send missionaries and support to various lands where significant needs exist. The opportunities vary: medical activity, educational programs, social service and evangelism. The primary goal, however, is to plant and develop local churches, and is ultimately to turn over to the nationals the function and control of their own churches. It is thrilling to see how many of these churches are developing strong abilities to reach out to unbelieving groups. Some are even sending their own missionaries to other countries.

Baptist fellowships also support home mission programs for the purpose of planting new churches and strengthening existing churches. We continue to find areas in our own country that are essentially untouched with the gospel. These must be reached in order to fulfill the commission given by our Lord. Along with that, some existing churches are struggling and faltering. Home missions programs enter into these situations to make possible new vitality and viability. A large part of this is accomplished through districts. These district organizations play an important role in the progress of the church in our own land.

A further work that is carried on by the larger fellowship

is education. Early on in the history of Baptists the need to train people for the work of the church was recognized. For example, the Baptist General Conference began an educational program in 1871 in Chicago. That was a seminary which was under the aegis of the Baptist Union Theological School, now the Divinity School of the University of Chicago. In 1914 the seminary moved permanently to St. Paul, Minnesota, where in 1905 an academy had started that continued until 1936. A junior college was launched in 1931, and a senior college started in 1947. Bethel College and Seminary are now located on an idyllic campus in Arden Hills, a suburb of St. Paul. An extension of the Seminary was begun in 1977 in San Diego and moved into its own building in 1990.

Cooperative work is also necessary in Christian education programs, specialized areas for youth, women and men, and in publishing as well as promotional concerns. These and similar large ministries could not possibly be adequately handled by one or even a few local churches. The denomination is vital to the strategic fulfillment of the great commission. We are grateful to God that local churches have responded to the need for fellowship and cooperative effort within New Testament principles.

The interdenominational level

The term ecumenical was almost a household word to most Christians a few years ago. In its best sense it means fellowship at the interdenominational level. The word "ecumenical" comes from a Greek word meaning the inhabited earth. Thus, it is often used to refer to a movement to unite Protestant and Orthodox church forces of the world, and more recently this included Roman Catholics as well. That union has not been accomplished, but discussions and activities continue seeking to bring it about. The late William Temple, Archbishop of Canterbury, spoke of the movement as "the great new fact of our age." We must face this great new fact and determine our position.

There are many Christian groups who are not Baptist with whom we may have a common bond on the essential issues of faith. Concerning union with others, we who seek to follow New Testament principles must raise questions to discover our position and the position of the other groups. There can be no fellowship where there is disagreement on essentials.

Where cooperation is a possibility, let's study some reasons for fellowship beyond our own denominational level.

First, the New Testament makes clear the *oneness of all who are in Christ Jesus*. Read the following verses: John 17:11, 21-23; Romans 12:4-5, as well as the verses in the preceding section. We cannot avoid the biblical emphasis on the oneness of believers. We are one with anyone who loves the Lord Jesus, no matter what fellowship group that person may be in. With such people we can cooperate in united service. But where there is denial of a basic tenet of faith, the fellowship does not exist. We believe that the basic authority for the church is the Scriptures. Where there is submission to the authority of the Scriptures as God's written revelation to man, we can have fellowship. Where Jesus Christ is believed as Redeemer and Lord of life, there we can have fellowship.

In the New Testament we find a unity, but not a uniformity. For example, Peter, John and Paul were quite different in temperament, but the message they taught and preached was basically the same. The unity of the New Testament is a spiritual, dynamic unity—but it may not eventuate in organizational uniformity. The greatest uniformity in the church developed in the Middle Ages, and yet during that period the church was weakest in its effect on lives.

We would not submit to a superchurch organization that would violate the authority of the Scriptures, but we can and should have fellowship with those of like mind on the essential issues.

Another reason for a true ecumenical movement among believers is the *need for a united witness*. Some people yearn for a united church because of fear. The Christian church is in an unfriendly world. On most continents it is a small minority within vast populations. Sometimes the unbelieving world charges that faith should produce unity among believers. There is some legitimacy to this. We should work toward a united witness with those of like faith for the sake of an impact for Christ. But we should not operate out of a fear of the dissolution of the church. Our Lord said, "I will build my church, and the gates of Hades will not overcome it." One man has said that if a religious survey had been taken in the Roman Empire in A.D. 65, it would have shown the following results: for Jupiter, 51 percent; for Zeus, 30 percent; for Mithra, about 9 percent; for others, about 9 percent and for Jesus about 1 percent or less. The church did not give up in the time of the apostle Paul with such terrific odds against it, and it will not stop now.

We believe in the significant impact of a united witness with those of like faith. Because of this, many churches of evangelical persuasion have united with the National Association of Evangelicals as a means to express this united witness. The Baptist General Conference is a member. The Baptist World Alliance similarly expresses the broader Baptist witness around the world. In Washington, D.C., a further united witness is borne in domestic and governmental affairs through the Baptist Joint Committee on Public Affairs. When issues involved in government decisions threaten to violate human liberties and demand expression of Christian convictions, there is no effective way of challenging these decisions apart from such a united voice.

Third is the *world need*. Some areas of world need can be met only through united fellowship. One of these is world relief. There are regions of the world that a group such as the National Association of Evangelicals or the Baptist World Alliance can go into that we could not reach alone as a denominational fellowship. Our overseas missionaries frequently need the help of a larger group in obtaining passports and visas or facing other issues that confront them. Often a denomination can enter a new mission field by cooperating with other groups who are already there. Through such cooperation more effective ministry takes place.

Fourth is our *concern for religious liberty*. Some nations of the world have suppressed the liberties of people under their rule. Some nations with a totalitarian government and others that are dominated by a particular religious group may deny freedoms to those of different persuasion. Those situations are of deep concern to Baptists. On many occasions representatives of the National Association of Evangelicals and the Baptist World Alliance have been able to bring about better arrangements for missionaries in some countries by working through the United States State Department. Persecutions have been stopped and confiscated properties have been returned because of this united voice. Oppression persists, so we continue to need this united testimony for freedom.

A final reason for working together is *that we might understand one another better.* In a shrinking world we must learn to live together. This is true in the religious world also. United activity helps us see our weaknesses and correct our failures. It gives us deeper convictions on our settled beliefs. It also makes us realize that there are those who love the Lord in other groups than ours. Such fellowship does not demand a compromise of essential convictions. If it does, we cannot have fellowship.

Many churches have discovered the value of cooperative efforts locally. Churches of various denominations cooperate during the summer in combined meetings. Throughout the school year several churches may cooperate in released time from public school for Christian education. In all of these instances there need be no compromise of essential convictions. These churches are learning to work together in the great task of serving Jesus Christ.

The day in which we live demands cooperation. We cannot adequately function in isolation. There are worldwide needs that can be met effectively only by a united voice. Local issues and problems demand cooperative effort. We need not violate our biblical convictions in such cooperation. In fact such fellowship is a response to a biblical emphasis on our oneness (John 10:16; 11:49-53).

12

The Nature of Our Worship

Practices of worship differ greatly among different denominations and within various groups. Many liturgical churches (which normally follow a prescribed litany) have become quite free in worship. Others, where freedom has been the norm, have become more liturgical. Experimentation in styles of worship has not been uncommon. All this expresses a deep yearning to find an experience of worship that is vital and real.

Because of the current interest in worship styles, let's rethink worship in the light of the New Testament. We find frequent expressions of worship in Jesus' day. For some, worship is a declaration of *thanksgiving* to the Lord for the benefits He has given. For some it is a matter of *asking in prayer*. Occasionally it is an utterance of fear. That was true, for instance, in the case of the demons possessing the maniac of Gadara. They were fearful in the Lord's presence. We do not worship in fear in that sense. The only fear we should have is an *awesome respect* for our Lord. *Adoration* also plays a part in New Testament worship.

We must notice the contrast between Old Testament worship and New Testament worship. We are a New Testament people, and thus we must guard our worship to be sure it is New Testament in form. In the New Testament there is a lack of emphasis on the external. No longer is the temple or the tabernacle central. Worship is now a direct relationship to God. There is a new sense of freedom in worship. The use of fixed forms is unnecessary. New Testament saints have found they can worship in the open air as well as in a sanctuary. Further, New Testament worship places more emphasis on the people and less on the leader than does the Old Testament. In the Old Testament we see little of the people's participation, but much of the priest's activity. This is not true in the New Testament.

With the New Testament era came a change of spirit. The worshipers of the early church were radiant. A new joy filled their lives. A further change was the new access of power not evident in the worship of the Old Testament. Now the individual had a power with God that transformed his life. All these differences changed worship.

Now you might ask, "What is worship?" There are many definitions, but I like the simple one that has been repeated in similar forms by various writers: "Worship is a person's response to God's revelation of Himself." That definition is simple, understandable and comprehensive. It involves God. It involves us. This is worship.

Worship consists of an objective part and a subjective part. The *objective* focuses attention upon God. The *subjective* refers to us and our response to God's message to us. In worship there is both a giving and a getting. We give adoration, reverence and thanksgiving. We receive a message from God when we are open and asking.

Today there is some confusion about the real meaning of worship. Christians yearn for a genuine experience of worship. Hopefully we can clarify its significance in a way that will make it vital. Our study in this chapter is based on John 4:7-26, where our Lord Himself instructs us in the real meaning of worship.

It is spiritual

In verses 23 and 24 we recognize that worship must be carried on in spirit and in truth. What does it mean to be spiritual in worship? Spiritual worship includes centering attention on God. Verse 24 says, "God is spirit." This is really the objective side of worship. A large part of worship should help us center our thoughts on the Lord. Read also Matthew 4:10; Philippians 3:3; Hebrews 11:6. Our thinking in worship should be primarily away from self.

How may we respond in this kind of worship? We express it in the *adoration* that most likely will come in the early part of the church's worship service. We may demonstrate our adoration in various ways. Some churches that conduct more than one morning service plan one with a contemporary emphasis and another in a more traditional mood. Others make each service the same. All leaders struggle with the most effective way to conduct worship that is consistent with biblical principles and also suits the needs of the people. The wishes of people can be quite varied. Older Christians tend to enjoy a traditional service that uses hymns and gospel songs. Many younger people think these stuffy and stilted and find meaning in praise choruses. We must recognize these differences and try to help Christians understand one another. If we have a right attitude toward God, we will have a right attitude toward ourselves and toward others. We need also to be aware of what appeals to the outsider. Since the church is concerned about outreach, we must be ready to use programs that attract the peripheral person. This can be done effectively in ways that are consistent with our definition of worship.

Remember, history is a story of change and adjustment. Many of the gospel songs that are so familiar to us began as a radical change in the latter part of the nineteenth century under the leadership of Ira D. Sankey. In the 1930s and '40s a new phenomenon took place in the use of gospel choruses and jingles. In each of these eras those who were comfortable with the status quo had a difficult time adjusting. The same is true today.

Praise choruses and gospel songs and hymns can all be used to adore and worship God. We must be open to the Spirit's prompting. Leadership is crucial in worship. Remember in the New Testament the emphasis is on the people's participation. Leaders must lead the people and not inject themselves too much into the worship. Congregational singing is participation time, not educational time. People learn by doing.

Prayer can also be a time of adoration of and reverence for God. Too often our understanding of prayer is self-centered. We feel it is only for asking the Lord to do something for us or give something to us. Prayer is vital when it focuses on God, who He is, what He means to us and what He has done for us.

Genuine worship is dynamic, vital and uplifting to the congregation.

It is direct

In John 4:20-21 we find that location is not the significant matter in worship. Attitude creates the atmosphere more than environment. One can worship God as truly in a tent as in a cathedral. Ask soldiers who have been out on the battlefield. Ask those who love the Lord and worshiped in a tent or out in the open air with just some rough logs to sit on. Did they sense the presence of God? They were in contact with God because their attitude created the atmosphere of worship.

I don't mean to minimize the significance of a good building to create a worshipful atmosphere, but this should not be our most important consideration. Real worship means direct access to and genuine communication with

God. Read Hebrews 10:19-25. The work of Jesus Christ has given the believer a direct access to God that no one ever possessed before. There is but one mediator between God and us, and that is Christ (1 Timothy 2:5). No other is able to provide an entrance into the presence of God.

Every person who leads in worship must aid those in the congregation to experience this direct access to God. This should be done even in our confession of sin. As we pray and confess our sin before God, everyone should be participating. This is further practiced in what we call the pastoral prayer. The prayer may be uttered by a pastor or another person. It is pastoral in that it is a shepherding or priestly act. In the Old Testament the priest represented the people before God. In the pastoral prayer the one praying is representing the people before God. In liturgical churches the pastor sometimes faces the altar during the prayer to express the priestly aspect in that he is representing the people before God. But we find in the New Testament that all believers are priests unto God (1 Peter 2:9; Revelation 1:6). In Baptist churches, therefore, the one praying does not turn his back to the congregation. He or she is one with the congregation and is praying for and with them. Every person enters into the prayer. This takes the place of sacrifice in the Old Testament. We give to the Lord our sacrifices of praise and thanksgiving.

The prayer will include *thanksgiving* for all God has done, *requests* for what is needed among the local people, and *intercession* for those who are not present—for absent members, for missionaries, the needs of the leaders of the land and the city and state governments. Adoration and confession need not come in this prayer since that has likely been covered earlier in the service.

The prayer will be specific. It will state definite things for which the church is thankful and requests and intercessions that they desire of God. Whoever leads in prayer should visualize needs that may be present in the congregation. There are many. A leader in prayer is likely in touch with people's needs and can pray for specific ones without mentioning names. Sometime universal needs common to us all can be mentioned. One man testified that he thrilled at listening to his pastor pray, for the pastor seemed to know exactly what his needs were.

Such praying requires preparation, and some of us in Baptist circles are a little disturbed about preparing to pray. I do not necessarily endorse reading prayers, but lack of preparation can be as great a violation of direct praying as mere reading; for we become victims of habit. We use phrases over and over again until they have no meaning. Preparation for public prayer will make that prayer direct and fresh and meaningful to all who participate.

It is intelligent

Worship is not to be a mystery. It is to be understood. Read John 4:22 and Acts 17:23. Far too many people worship in mystery. The new mood in architecture is changing that by seeking to avoid mystery and to emphasize understanding. Church buildings are much plainer, with emphasis on congregational participation and involvement. Many churches are built "in the round," with the pulpit in the center, emphasizing the concern for understanding. Some liturgical churches put the altar in the midst of the congregation. Cardinal Montini said, "Liturgy is for men, not men for liturgy." Though it was not this way through most of church history, the concern for intelligent worship is part of the contemporary church.

People who participate in worship must find it intelligible to them. This is the primary reason Baptists usually have a central pulpit. Our emphasis is on the Bible. We are a people of a Book. We believe that God has given a written revelation to point us to the Living Revelation, Jesus Christ. We believe that the Bible should be central so that we might be an understanding people.

Since the Bible is central in our worship, Scripture reading is significant. We do not include Scripture reading in the worship service just to take up time. God has given this revelation to be read. Those who read it ought to read it in the best way possible. In this respect we have frequently been very shabby. All those who read the Scriptures publicly ought to prepare in advance and know what they are reading so they will read understandably.

Because of the importance of the Bible in worship, the congregation should listen thoughtfully as Scripture is read. We must develop the skill of listening carefully and intelligently. In some congregations many carry their Bibles to church and follow the reading. If that is true, the reader should give time for the congregation to turn to the location after the text is announced. All that needs to be announced is the starting place of the reading to avoid confusion. Many prefer watching the reader and listening carefully. In either case the reading should be done with clarity and meaningful emphasis. The listener should give studied attention to the reading so understanding comes.

We believe that the preaching of the Word is the prophetic task today. The minister of the gospel is God's prophet. Read 1 Corinthians 1:21. The sincere minister of the gospel may not be a tremendous orator, but the preacher will plan with sincere prayer, meditation and hard work in the preparation of sermons. The pastor will make the most of clearly presenting God's message to the people for that hour.

This places a high responsibility not only on the pastor, but also on the people—for it is the people's responsibility to enter into worship and into the preaching in the light of intelligent worship. It means that people must pray much that their pastor will be God's voice in the pulpit. It will mean that people must refrain from criticism of the pastor that might harm the message in the minds of others. One who is lost and needs the Lord might grasp this criticism and miss an opportunity to find Christ. If there is error, if the pastor misses the mark, then the elders, deacons or church members can quietly consult with their minister. It is the responsibility of the people in the congregation to encourage others to listen carefully to the message of God's Word, for this is God's message. We must heed it.

A further matter in intelligent worship is the use of music. First of all, we must choose good music. Good music may include all types: the praise chorus, the gospel song, the hymn and the anthem. The content will convey a message that contributes to intelligent worship. This demands hard work in preparation by the choir, worship team and all who participate. Only the best will be used for the Lord. I am not saying that only professional musicians should perform, but much effort should be expended in the best possible preparation. It is most important that anyone singing will seek to communicate a message. Music just for the sake of music is not sufficient. Music is a God-given vehicle for expressing truth, and we need to use it that way. This must be emphasized over and over again, whether for the choir, worship team or soloist. Music serves to aid worshipers in intelligent participation in worship.

It is sincere

Reread John 4:23-24, noticing the emphasis on truth. There must be sincerity in worship or it cannot be real worship. Sincerity concerns the more subjective part in worship. It is interesting to note that the word sincere is an Anglicized Latin term meaning "without wax." It might seem at first as though there is no connection between the two terms, but we are told that in Roman times artisans produced a fine porcelain which was greatly valued and brought a very high price. The porcelain was so fragile that it easily cracked when it was fired. Dishonest dealers were in the habit of filling in the cracks with a pearly white wax that looked enough like the true porcelain to pass without being readily detected in the shop. If it was held to the light, however, the wax at once appeared as a dark seam. The honest Roman dealers marked their wares *sine cera,* meaning without wax. Thus, sincere worshipers are those who can be held up to the sun and tested. They will be found honest and pure before God.

In Matthew 15:9 the Lord denounced the Pharisees who did not worship in sincerity. Sincerity expresses itself in an openness to God and His message for our lives. Whispering or being occupied with other things should not be part of the mature Christian's worship. This is especially true during prayer. Some seem undisturbed about looking around or doing something else while someone is leading in prayer. This violates sincere worship. There may be emergencies, such as caring for children, that demand attention. This is understandable. But sincere worship presupposes an openness to God in every part of the service.

Sincere worship also includes dedication of the individual to the Lord. This may be expressed in several parts of a service. When we give our offering according to the will of the Lord, we are dedicating ourselves to Him in worship. Failing to do the will of God is failing in dedication. As a leader prays everyone participates in a sense of dedication.

The close of the service is particularly a time of dedication. Throughout the hour of worship each worshiper has met with God. He has observed Him in adoration, in praise, in prayer and in hearing God's message. Now is the time for him to commit himself to the Lord. This is usually done in quiet moments at the close of the service. Then each individual rededicates himself to Jesus Christ. Sometimes when the Christian has deviated from the path of God and has sinned against Him, it is necessary to publicly express a new beginning. There are various ways that such expression may be shown. In some churches a public invitation is given for people making some type of decision to come to the front of the church. Many prefer a more quiet way. It may occur with an individual counselor or in some type of support group.

The nature of true worship demands response on the part of the worshipers. When God is present, when His message is heard and discovered, a worshiper must respond in some way. Response may be quiet. It may be within one's own thought life. Response may be part of a process of growth, or it may be a crisis decision that demands a more dramatic expression of the decision one has made.

13

Church History at a Glance

Baptists claim to be New Testament people. Their churches arose because of biblical teachings. We believe there has been a stream of people from the days of the apostles who have sought to remain true to the New Testament, but Baptists claim no strict apostolic succession. We cannot trace our history in strict historical fashion back to New Testament days. Our roots come out of the Reformation period like other Protestants, but Baptist churches as such have existed only since about 1610.

Persecutions

In the time of the early church, Christians met first in homes. As the groups grew in size, larger buildings were needed. Persecution followed the early worshipers of Christ. Persecution of Christians in the days of the New Testament led to a spread of the gospel to many other cities beyond Jerusalem. The apostle Paul reached many more areas because of opposition than he would have without it.

Christians endured severe persecution for the first three centuries of their activity. They were oppressed by the Jews and by the Romans. Some of the emperors, like Nero and

Diocletian, took special delight in mistreating the Christians and seeking to destroy them. Diocletian boasted that he had done away with the Christians. These persecutions merely fanned the enthusiasm of the early Christians until they literally conquered the Empire.

The Dark Ages

In A.D. 313 Emperor Constantine made an alliance between the church and the state. He professed to be a Christian. Some question whether he was a genuine believer, because he used the church to conquer more lands for his empire. Many evils followed this alliance of church and state. Each city had a separate bishop or pastor of the church. With this union of church and state the power of the bishop of Rome increased continuously for the next thousand years. His power overshadowed that of the bishops of other cities. It looked like a good day for the Christian church, but instead that period ushered in the Dark Ages.

These centuries saw the greatest uniformity in the church, but it was also the era when the church made the least impact upon human life. During this time many unscriptural teachings were added to church doctrine. Some of those teachings were prayers for the dead, adoration of Mary, worship of saints and images and teaching the concept of purgatory. It was also during this period that the Bible was taken away from lay people and tradition was made equal in authority to the Bible. The practice of buying forgiveness for sins, known as indulgences, also began. The church developed an unholy desire for wealth, luxury and power that gradually caused it to lose its spiritual influence.

The Reformation

Even in this period known as the Dark Ages, the Lord had His witnesses. The purest teachings of the Bible were found in the despised sects and among those who were called heretics. There was a growing unrest in many sections about the unspiritual character of the church. This finally led to the explosion that occurred on October 31, 1517, when Martin Luther nailed his 95 theses (protests against unscriptural teachings and practices) on the door of his church.

Baptists came from the Reformation that was led by Luther and other Reformers. Other church leaders sought to bring reform long before Luther arrived on the scene. I will just mention a few of these. One was Arnold of Brescia, from a city in northern Italy. A priest in that city, he tried to institute reform by denouncing the sins of the clergy. He insisted on a spiritual church with a converted membership. He also taught, amazingly enough, the separation of church and state. Because of his teachings he was finally hanged on the gallows in Rome in 1155.

Peter Waldo, the founder of the Waldensians, was another of these reformers. He had been a wealthy merchant in Lyons, France, but felt called to take up a life of poverty. In a short time a group of disciples followed his unselfish service, daily preaching the gospel. Among their tenets of faith were: 1) obedience to the Scriptures, rather than the Pope; 2) a repudiation of the sacrifice of the mass and the unscriptural doctrines of purgatory and confession; 3) a rejection of indulgences; 4) the right of all laymen and laywomen to preach. Waldo lived in the last part of the twelfth century.

Another of these earlier reformers, John Wycliffe, a scholar from England, translated the Bible into English. He emphasized a literal interpretation of the Scriptures, giving the Scriptures to the people in their own language and he rejected the doctrine of transubstantiation. Wycliffe lived at the end of the fourteenth century. His influence touched Europe through the teachings of John Huss of Bohemia. Huss was a priest who preached against the sins of the clergy and insisted upon the use of the Scriptures by the people, which the Pope had openly opposed in 1409. Found guilty of heresy on July 6, 1415, he was burned at the stake. He died exhorting the people from the Scriptures and singing a hymn.

These were some of the forerunners of the Reformation. The Reformation led by Luther, Calvin, Zwingli and others opposed the corrupt practices of the Roman Catholic Church that were in contradiction to the Scriptures. They believed the Bible should be in the language of the people. The movement caught fire and spread rapidly across the continent of Europe and in a different way into England.

Anabaptists

It was during the Reformation that the Anabaptists began to make their impact felt. The name means "rebaptizers" and was given to the people who insisted on believer's baptism. It was in Switzerland that the Anabaptists first became influential. They followed Zwingli's leadership in the earlier days. One of the followers was Conrad Grebel, who became the founder of Anabaptism. The Anabaptists finally broke with Zwingli in 1523 when he compromised his reform by yielding to a state church system in Zurich.

The Anabaptists insisted upon believer's baptism and thus rejected infant baptism. They believed the Bible was the final authority for the life of the church. They also opposed the union of state and church and believed that church membership was only for the regenerate. Anabaptists were severely persecuted. This is understandable because even the great Reformers—Luther, Calvin and

Zwingli—maintained the ideas of infant baptism along with a state church. In the minds of the Anabaptists these positions were contrary to New Testament teachings.

The Anabaptists became the forerunners of our present Baptist movement. An outstanding early Anabaptist was Balthaser Hubmaier (1480-1528). He was a Roman Catholic priest in Waldshut, Austria, who believed that faith in Jesus Christ must precede baptism and that religion was a voluntary matter not to be forced upon an individual. He also believed that the Scriptures alone ought to be the standard and rule for Christians. He was burned at the stake for his teachings, and his wife was drowned in the Danube. Such was the fate of many Anabaptists during this period.

The first actual Baptist church began under the leadership of John Smyth of England. With a group of congregational separatists who were forced to leave England because of their views, he went to Amsterdam, Holland, and formed a Baptist church in about 1608. (Baptist churches may have existed earlier in England, but that has not been clearly verified.) In about 1610 part of the group returned to England where Baptist churches began to spread. They were a persecuted group of people until 1689 when the Act of Toleration was passed.

Baptists in the United States

We now turn to the United States and find the beginning of Baptist work in 1639 in Providence, R.I. Roger Williams, a pastor in Plymouth Colony, Mass., came to believe that government should not interfere with the church. His teaching was contrary to the practices of the early colonists. They had fled from England and Europe to have religious freedom for themselves. But when they arrived on this continent, they refused to extend this freedom to others. They banished Roger Williams from their colony because of his views. In the dead of winter, January 1636, Williams plunged through the wilderness. His life was saved by friendly Indians whom he had previously helped in missionary endeavors. In Providence, in 1638, he led in the formation of a colony that gave complete liberty to all, no matter what their religious belief. In 1639 he espoused Baptist views and was baptized by immersion. Ten others were then baptized to form the First Baptist Church of Providence, which exists to this day.

This was only the beginning of religious freedom in North America. Much bloodshed and persecution was endured in most of the 13 colonies to give us the freedom we enjoy today. Baptists were hunted and molested, whipped, imprisoned, fined and publicly disgraced in every conceivable manner. For example, parents in the colony of Virginia were heavily fined for refusing to have their infants baptized. Yet with all that persecution, by 1740 there were 47 Baptist churches.

Baptist influence

Religious freedom as we know it in the United States today is largely a result of Baptist influence. The American Bill of Rights came about in large part through the democratic practices and beliefs of the Baptists of Virginia. Other religious groups who came to this continent did not hold to a complete freedom for all persons regardless of religious belief, nor did they support a complete separation of state and church.

A "Great Awakening" began in 1740 after George Whitefield came to this continent in 1739. His preaching, along with that of other revivalists, led to conversions in most of the towns of the colonies. The awakening did more for Baptist growth than anything else could have done. Baptist churches began to increase rapidly.

By 1792 there were 471 Baptist churches with 35,000 members in the U.S. By 1800 membership had reached 100,000, climbing to 4,000,000 by 1900 and 14,000,000 by 1945. According to Baptist World Alliance statistics, in 1993 more than 30,755,000 Baptists could be counted in North America and more than 38,100,000 worldwide. These statistics do not include members of several Baptist groups who are not aligned with the Alliance.

Baptists have made outstanding contributions to the spiritual progress of the world. The first modern world missionary was William Carey, a Baptist from England. The first American overseas missionary was Adoniram Judson, a Baptist. John Bunyan, author of the famous book, *Pilgrim's Progress,* was a Baptist pastor. The British and Foreign Bible Society was founded by John Hughes, another Baptist. According to some the greatest preacher since Paul the apostle, Charles Haddon Spurgeon, was a Baptist as was the prince of Bible expositors, Alexander Maclaren. The hymn "America" was written by a Baptist, Samuel F. Smith. The first Sunday school in America was founded in the First Baptist Church of Philadelphia in 1815.

The Baptist General Conference

There are several different Baptist conventions in the United States. We will look at a brief history of one of these. The Baptist General Conference is the title used to designate one fellowship of several hundred Baptist churches united to carry out the Lord's commission. This conference had its rise among Swedish immigrants and began on August 13, 1852, in Rock Island, Ill. Gustaf Palmquist had come to this area as a Lutheran pastor. Through a study of the Scriptures he embraced Baptist convictions and was baptized by immersion and ordained to the Baptist ministry in First Baptist Church of Galesburg, Ill., an American

Baptist church. Seven weeks later, in August 1852, three others were baptized to form the First Swedish Baptist church of America. In two years this group grew to between 40 and 50 members. More churches soon began in Village Creek, Iowa, New Sweden, Maine, New York City, Chicago, Moline, Ill., and other places.

F.O. Nilsson immigrated to the U.S. in 1854 to aid in the Baptist work. In 1834, as a 25-year-old sailor from Sweden, he had come to know Christ in New York City. Thirteen years later he was baptized by immersion in Germany. He returned to Sweden to lead in Baptist work, but was banished in 1851. He then came to Illinois to help in the missionary labors among the Swedish people. Later, through his efforts and those of others, churches were organized in Burlington, Iowa, as well as at Houston, Scandia, Chisago Lake and Carver, all in Minnesota.

The beginnings of Baptist General Conference work were slow. By 1864 there were only eleven churches with 360 members. Later the work began to grow more rapidly. A chart of growth from 1852 to 1952 may be found in *A Centenary History* by Adolf Olson, page 609. More recent growth and development is described in *Fifteen Eventful Years,* a 1961 publication of the Conference's Harvest Publications, *The 1970s in the Ministry of the Baptist General Conference,* and *The 1980s in the Ministry of the Baptist General Conference.*

A turning point in the life of the Baptist General Conference came in 1944 when the fellowship voted to launch its own world missions program. Before this time missionaries went out under the American Baptist Foreign Mission Society or independent mission boards. With this foreign missions decision, the Baptist General Conference severed its organizational ties with other conventions.

This advance in missions sparked advances in every other branch of Conference work and fostered a new enthusiasm in evangelism and in every aspect of local church activity. Church membership grew from 40,000 in 1944 to 142,000 members in 2000. From 288 churches, the Conference grew to about 900, with many new churches beginning each year.

As we conclude our study, let's remind ourselves of the importance of the Bible. It is our authority. It is the basis of our faith and life. We are who we are as Christians because of what we understand from the Scriptures. The more we reflect on the various doctrines and life issues in the Bible, the more we become convinced Baptist people. We have a great heritage and an exciting fellowship of people around the world. I hope you feel the same.

Baptists throughout their history have utilized doctrinal statements or affirmations of faith to declare their understanding of the teachings of the Bible. Since Baptists are non-creedal, such statements do not have ultimate authority. On the other hand, they are often used as a means of judging the viability of a church's membership in a convention and also for determining a leader's qualifications for serving in an official capacity. One such affirmation is included here.

An affirmation of faith
Adopted by the Baptist General Conference in 1951

1. THE WORD OF GOD
We believe that the Bible is the Word of God, fully inspired and without error in the original manuscripts, written under the inspiration of the Holy Spirit, and that it has supreme authority in all matters of faith and conduct.

2. THE TRINITY
We believe that there is one living and true God, eternally existing in three persons; that these are equal in every divine perfection, and that they execute distinct but harmonious offices in the work of creation, providence and redemption.

3. GOD THE FATHER
We believe in God the Father, an infinite, personal spirit, perfect in holiness, wisdom, power and love. We believe that He concerns Himself mercifully in the affairs of men, that He hears and answers prayers, and that He saves from sin and death all who come to Him through Jesus Christ.

4. JESUS CHRIST
We believe in Jesus Christ, God's only begotten Son, conceived by the Holy Spirit. We believe in His virgin

birth, sinless life, miracles and teachings. We believe in His substitutionary atoning death, bodily resurrection, ascension into heaven, perpetual intercession for His people, and personal visible return to earth.

5. THE HOLY SPIRIT

We believe in the Holy Spirit who came forth from the Father and Son to convict the world of sin, righteousness and judgment, and to regenerate, sanctify and empower all who believe in Jesus Christ. We believe that the Holy Spirit indwells every believer in Christ, and that He is an abiding helper, teacher and guide.

6. REGENERATION

We believe that all men are sinners by nature and by choice and are, therefore, under condemnation. We believe that those who repent of their sins and trust in Jesus Christ as Savior are regenerated by the Holy Spirit.

7. THE CHURCH

We believe in the universal church, a living spiritual body of which Christ is the head and all regenerated persons are members. We believe in the local church, consisting of a company of believers in Jesus Christ, baptized on a credible profession of faith, and associated for worship, work and fellowship. We believe that God has laid upon the members of the local church the primary task of giving the gospel of Jesus Christ to a lost world.

8. CHRISTIAN CONDUCT

We believe that Christians should live for the glory of God and the well-being of others; that their conduct should be blameless before the world; that they should be faithful stewards of their possessions; and that they should seek to realize for themselves and others the full stature of maturity in Christ.

9. THE ORDINANCES

We believe that our Lord Jesus Christ has committed two ordinances to the local church: baptism and the Lord's Supper. We believe that Christian baptism is the immersion of a believer in water into the name of the triune God. We believe that the Lord's Supper was instituted by Christ for commemoration of His death. We believe that these two ordinances should be observed and administered until the return of the Lord Jesus Christ.

10. RELIGIOUS LIBERTY

We believe that every human being has direct relations with God, and is responsible to God alone in all matters of faith; that each church is independent and must be free from interference by any ecclesiastical or political authority; that therefore Church and State must be kept separate as having different functions, each fulfilling its duties free from dictation or patronage of the other.

11. CHURCH COOPERATION

We believe that local churches can best promote the cause of Jesus Christ by cooperating with one another in a denominational organization. Such an organization, whether a regional or a district conference, exists and functions by the will of the churches. Cooperation in a conference is voluntary and may be terminated at any time. Churches may likewise cooperate with interdenominational fellowships on a voluntary independent basis.

12. THE LAST THINGS

We believe in the personal and visible return of the Lord Jesus Christ to earth and the establishment of His kingdom. We believe in the resurrection of the body, the final judgment, the eternal felicity of the righteous, and the endless suffering of the wicked.

Bibliography

Anderson, Donald E., ed., *The 1970s in the Ministry of the Baptist General Conference* and *The 1980s in the Ministry of the Baptist General Conference* (Arlington Heights, IL: Harvest Publications, 1981, 233 pp.). An updating of the life and ministry of various aspects of the Baptist General Conference.

Anderson, Leith, *A Church for the 21st Century* (Minneapolis: Bethany House Publishers, 1992, 250 pp.). A practical grappling with the changes we face to make the church effective in our time.

Anderson, Leith, *Dying for Change* (Minneapolis: Bethany House Publishers, 1990, 208 pp.). Keen insight into the societal, spiritual and leadership changes that the church needs to face.

Barna, George, *The Frog in the Kettle* (Ventura, CA: Regal Books, 1990, 235 pp.). Because the radical changes that are happening are coming subtly and imperceptibly, the church must be alerted in order to be effective. This book helps us.

Barna, George, *User Friendly Churches* (Ventura, CA: Regal Books, 1991., 191 pp.). A practical approach to utilizing the key characteristics and attitudes that successful churches have in common.

Colson, Charles, *The Body: Being Light in Darkness* (Dallas, TX: Word Publishing, 1992, 455 pp.). A well-balanced treatment of the doctrines of the church for our day. A classic.

Guston, David and Erikson, Martin, eds., *Fifteen Eventful Years* (Evanston, IL: Harvest Publications, 1961, 231 pp.). A careful survey of the various ministries of the Baptist General Conference in the crucial years of advance — 1945-1960.

Kuen, Alfred F., *I Will Build My Church* (Chicago: Moody Press, 1971, 366 pp.). Translated from the French, it subjects the controversies and problems of the church to the authority of the Bible.

Lumpkin, William, *Baptist Confessions of Faith* (Valley Forge, PA: Judson Press, 1959, 439 pp.). A collection of seventeenth- through twentieth-century statements of faith, including documents discovered since 1910.

Maring, Norman H. and Hudson, Winthrop S., *A Baptist Manual of Polity and Practice* (Valley Forge, PA: Judson Press, 1958). A Baptist manual written by two church historians.

McBeth, H. Leon, *The Baptist Heritage: Four Centuries of Baptist Witness* (Nashville: Broadman Press, 1987, 822 pp.). A comprehensive history of Baptist movements from the 1600s through 1980s, covering individuals and the rise of institutions.

Newton, Louie D., *Why I Am a Baptist* (Boston: Beacon Press, 1965, 306 pp.). A Baptist response to a series by leading churchmen of other denominations.

Olson, Adolf, *A Centenary History* (Chicago: Baptist Conference Press, 1952, 635 pp.). A definitive history of the Baptist General Conference of America.

Ortlund, Raymond C., *Let the Church Be the Church* (Waco, TX: Word Books, 1983, 122 pp.). An anecdotal and scriptural approach to seeing what God intended the church to be.

Snyder, Howard A., *The Community of the King* (Downers Grove, IL: InterVarsity Press, 1977, 216 pp.). Sets forth a theology of the church and gives practical guidelines for church growth and life.

Snyder, Howard A., *Liberating the Church* (Downers Grove, IL: InterVarsity Press, 1983, 288 pp.). Looks at the church as sacrament, community, servant and witness, and discusses Kingdom ministry, theology, Scripture and lifestyle.

Snyder, Howard A., *The Problem of Wine Skins* (Downers Grove, IL: InterVarsity Press, 1975, 214 pp.). Faces the kinds of church systems which are most compatible with the gospel in our modern techno-urban society.